WORLD TOURISM ORGANIZATION

Making Tourism Work for Small Island Developing States

srh

Berlin University of Applied Sciences

Träger: SRH Hochschulen Berlin GmbH

Department of Sustainable Development of Tourism

Making Tourism Work for Small Island Developing States
ISBN 92-844-0782-6

Published and printed by the World Tourism Organization, Madrid, Spain
First printing in 2004

World Tourism Organization
Calle Capitán Haya, 42
28020 Madrid, Spain
Tel.: (+34) 915 678 100
Fax: (+34) 915 713 733
Web site: www.world-tourism.org
Email: omt@world-tourism.org

Table of Contents

 - ISBN 92-844-0782-6

Acknowledgement

This report has been prepared for The World Tourism Organization by Ms. Zoritsa Urosevic, Tourism Consultant and Member of the WTO Programme Committee, under the supervision of Mr. Eugenio Yunis, Head, Sustainable Development of Tourism Department, WTO. Mr. Philippe Lemaistre, Programme Officer at the same Department, reviewed draft texts, tables and final editing of the report.

Preface

The World Tourism Organization, in its new capacity as the UN specialized agency in the field of Tourism, is pleased to contribute with this study to the ten-year review of the Barbados Programme of Action (BPOA +10). Since BPOA +10 will examine the development of Small Island Developing States, it is essential that tourism is included in the equation.

International tourism to SIDS represents 3.7% of the world total or more than 26 million tourists in 2003. For most islands, tourism is the main economic activity in terms of income generation, employment creation, and foreign exchange earnings. In many SIDS, tourism is a substantive contributor to GDP.

But due to their small size, islands are quite vulnerable to the negative environmental and social impacts that tourism can sometimes bring. That is why it is vital to plan, manage and monitor tourism development in SIDS, aiming at sustainability objectives. To do so, island destinations need the economic and technical support of international organizations.

This WTO report, *Making Tourism Work for SIDS*, presents a summary of the current status of tourism in SIDS, while providing evidence of the key importance it has for the sustainable development of many islands and for the achievement of the UN Millennium Development Goals. It also addresses the key issues that need to be considered by small island nations in order for the tourism industry to be more sustainable in the long term.

Francesco Frangialli
Secretary-General

Introduction

Tourism at the crossroads of economic, social and environmental considerations

"Small Island Developing States, and islands supporting small communities are a special case both for environment and development. They are ecologically fragile and vulnerable. Their small size, limited resources, geographic dispersion and isolation from markets, place them at a disadvantage economically and prevent economies of scale"

Agenda 21

Agenda 21, the Barbados Programme of Action (BPOA) for the Sustainable Development of Small Island Developing States (SIDS), and the World Summit on Sustainable Development (WSSD), all underscored that small island states are faced with the greatest complexities and challenges of sustainable development.

The WSSD in 2002 addressed the special issues of SIDS in the Johannesburg Plan of Implementation by setting forth a number of targets and timetables related to SIDS. It also called for a review of the implementation of the 1994 Barbados Programme of Action for the Sustainable Development of Small Island Developing States leading to an international meeting in Mauritius in January 2005.

The inadequate attention paid to genuine sustainability in areas where tourism growth is significant or where natural, cultural and heritage conditions are particularly vulnerable was emphasized in Johannesburg where, for the first time, tourism was clearly included in the agenda and several paragraphs of the Plan of Implementation were adopted by the Summit.

Since its foundation in 1975, the World Tourism Organization has been assisting developing countries to strengthen their national and local economies through tourism. Today the central issues in the work of the Organization have become the reduction of poverty through the sustainable development of tourism and the integration of the UN Millennium Development Goals in what is today a pivotal sector of the world economy.

Working in close collaboration with the United Nations as an affiliated agency since 1977, the World Tourism Organization has been designated by the UN General Assembly, in December 2003 as the new UN specialized agency responsible for tourism.

By virtue of this agreement, the UN have signified that tourism has an equal footing with such other principal activities of human society as industry, agriculture, transport, education, culture, health, and labour. This new status in the UN will call for close and continuous coordination among the different bodies and agencies of the United Nations system under the supervision of ECOSOC.

This report intends to demonstrate the importance of tourism in SIDS and the need to support its sustainable development by both, governments and international and bilateral development assistance agencies. It provides policy orientations, guidelines and other tools to the NTAs, the tourism industry and other tourism stakeholders in SIDS on how to develop and manage tourism in a sustainable manner for the benefit of their population.

Executive Summary

Journey on a fragile planet

"By its very nature, sustainable development is a process of transformation in which the exploitation of resources, the selection of investments, the orientation of techniques and institutional change take place in harmony, strengthening present and future potential...".
1987 Brundtland / United Nations / "Our Common Future".

We live on a fragile planet that needs to be looked after. This is the concern behind the "sustainable development" concept defined in Rio de Janeiro in 1992.

In the context of the BPOA, a review of progress in the Implementation of the Programme of Action for the Sustainable Development of Small Island Developing States leads us here to examine the vital contribution that international tourism is making to the economic, social, environmental and cultural progress of mankind and in safeguarding world peace.

According to the World Tourism Organization definition, sustainable tourism development and management refer to the environmental, economic and socio-cultural aspects of tourism, with the establishment of a suitable balance between these three dimensions to guarantee its long-term sustainability. Thus, sustainable tourism should make optimal use of environmental resources that constitute a key element in tourism development, respect the socio-cultural authenticity of host communities, and ensure viable, long-term economic operations, providing social and economic benefits to all stakeholders and contributing to poverty alleviation.

Tourism is not merely a major economic sector and one of the mainstays of international trade. Its role in environmental protection, in preserving biodiversity, in conserving the cultural heritage, in promoting mutual understanding among peoples and peace among nations is highly significant.

Achieving sustainable tourism is a continuous process and it requires constant monitoring of impacts, introducing the necessary preventive and corrective measures. Due to their small size, islands are quite vulnerable from both an environmental and a social point of view. No other economic activity cuts across so many sectors, levels and interests as tourism, so there is a vital need to integrate planning for tourism with national development and resource management plans, as well as measuring tourism socio-economic costs and benefits. Sustainable tourism should also maintain a high level of tourist satisfaction and ensure a meaningful experience to the tourists, raising their awareness about sustainability issues.

As one of the most successful export industries in the world, international tourism has become the main economic activity for many island nations - in terms of both income and employment generation, its contribution to gross domestic product, and its substantial impact on the balance of payment, trade and foreign exchange earnings. However, the challenging international economic conditions resulting from globalization increases the vulnerability of nearly all SIDS in their prospects for the future.

SIDS have performed particularly well in tourism over the last ten or fifteen years against other sectors.. Between 1990 and 2002, while the average annual rate of total international tourist arrivals worldwide grew by 3.7%, some island states saw their arrivals grow at much faster annual rates, such as Maldives (9.1%) and Dominican Republic (8.6%).

Tourism growth, while much desired, also brings with it new challenges. SIDS that are trying to strengthen their tourism development have an overriding concern with problems which limit tourism growth in the short term - mainly air access, capital investment and infrastructure development. Besides, pressure on the environment and local communities is increased, requiring a certain number of rules and principles. With the weak institutional capacity of most SIDS, minimizing those impacts would require the establishment of an appropriate framework as well as initiatives aimed at building a wider, more sustainable base of support for tourism, with the promotion of a sense of ownership in order to ensure the success of the industry.

Considered as one of the most successful nature-based industries, tourism is as well a consumer of natural resources. Tourism should be seen as instrumental in conserving biodiversity, on account of its being managed in a sustainable manner.

For Small Island Developing States, the search for sustainability begins at the crossroads of a triple concern involving economic, social and environmental considerations. The quest for economic development without which little else is possible, the quest for greater social justice and the quest for protection and renewal of natural resources that cannot last forever.

This report, built upon the various areas of activity of WTO and especially those concerning the sustainable development of tourism, will help to establish the necessary links between tourism on the one hand, and each of the other priority areas established in the BPOA that impinge on tourism or vice-versa.

The aim is to examine the various areas that need to be considered by governments and the private sector if they wish tourism to contribute successfully to the overall economic, social and environmental sustainability of their territories. A set of WTO recommendations, existing guidelines, key measures, policies and new initiatives are presented in the context of SIDS such as the Tourism Satellite Account, guiding principles for sustainable tourism development for SIDS, Sustainable Tourism Indicators, certification issues, the Global Code of Ethics for Tourism and Sustainable Tourism for the Elimination of Poverty (ST-EP Programme).

With these guidelines and tools, WTO intends to assist governments and other stakeholders in SIDS in their efforts to develop a tourism industry that is sustainable in the long term, maximizing the social and economic benefits and reducing the negative impacts on the environment of Small Island Developing States.

WTO believes that tourism, if it grows sustainably and if it delivers real benefits to the peoples of the developing world, can help island nations in their approach to achieving the Millennium Development Goals.

Chapter 1

Tourism in SIDS: A key economic sector

For many islands, tourism has become the main economic activity over the last fifteen years, in terms of both income and employment generation. Due to their small size, islands are quite vulnerable from both an environmental and a social point of view. This vulnerability may put at risk the long-term sustainability of tourism-based economic development of the islands, if tourism is not appropriately planned, developed and managed.

Because of their geographical isolation and resource limitations SIDS face enormous difficulties when developing their economies. Land is the scarcest resource and few island nations have sufficient natural resources to develop industries such as mining or agriculture or a manufacturing base to a scale that would make them economically viable or to provide significant economic revenues for the local economy.

Small Island Developing States are the most challenged entities when it comes to developing large-scale industries that can provide maximum economic benefits with minimum use of resources. Furthermore, most SIDS are heavily dependent on imports for their daily needs, which increases the degree of leakages in their economies, and they are even further challenged, since each island has to be self sufficient in terms of energy, freshwater, sewage treatment and solid waste disposal.

Tourism is an expanding sector with broad opportunities for island development. Sustainable island development depends on an ability to manage island resources on an overall basis to ensure their conservation and the preservation of the island's human, economic, natural, and cultural heritage. Given the close interrelationships among all these factors on islands and tourism's potentially polarizing force, development of the tourism sector will only have a solid foundation and a generally positive influence to the extent that it is economically viable, ecologically bearable, and socially acceptable.

1.1 International Tourism

International Tourism ranks in the top five exports categories in the world. Since the 1960's, tourism has been growing at very high annual rates, except for the last three years, when political instability and terrorism have made tourism more vulnerable. However, these external shocks have as well highlighted how much tourism is vital for SIDS in terms of their overall economic performance. WTO has played an instrumental role during these years of crises in establishing a network and a working committee (Recovery Committee) as well as a quarterly publication compiled by the WTO's Marketing Intelligence Department (Tourism Barometer), to share information, assist and guide member states to face and overcome the crises. Since 2004, an increase in tourist arrivals at most destinations, including islands, shows that the **vulnerability of tourism is coupled with resilience**. The growing importance of tourism in SIDS takes place within a general, sustained growth of tourist movements worldwide.

International tourist arrivals have grown from a mere 25 million in 1950 to 456 million in 1990 and to over 700 million in 2002. This represents an average annual growth rate close to 3.7% over the last 12 years, with receipts generated growing at a higher rate than that of arrivals.

But more important than this growth has been the diversification of destinations that has taken place during the last years. While in 1970 fifteen countries, all of them from Europe plus USA and Canada, accounted for 75% of total international tourist arrivals, in 2002, their share of the market had fallen to 60%. In parallel, many developing countries saw their tourist arrivals increase significantly, including several island states.

Benefiting from this diversification, many SIDS have performed particularly well over the last ten or fifteen years. While total international tourist arrivals worldwide grew at an average annual rate of 3.7% between 1990 and 2002, island states saw their arrivals grow at much faster annual rates, such as Cuba (18.2%), Cape Verde (13.2%), Maldives (9.1%), Dominican Republic (8.6%), Mauritius (8.4%), or Samoa (6.2%), to name but a few.

Tourism is by far the fastest-growing economic sector in all SIDS regions. Earnings from tourism as a proportion of total exports value exceeded 20% in 19 SIDS, 30% in 13, and 40% in 8. In Antigua the proportion is 86%, in Bahamas 84%, St Lucia 75%, Maldives 70%, Barbados 59% and St Kitts and Nevis 52%.

The forecasting study conducted by the World Tourism Organization to examine how the tourism industry, and particularly tourism demand, is likely to evolve in the next twenty years provides a valuable framework to the discussion about sustainability in tourism. The results indicate that international tourist arrivals are likely to increase at an annual average rate of around 4 per cent, to reach nearly 1.5 billion by the year 2020.

At the turn of the Millennium tourism has become one of the most dynamic industries in the world. It is therefore no wonder that a number of island nations have identified tourism as a vehicle for socio-economic growth and poverty reduction.

1.2 Tourism contribution in SIDS performances

Since the adoption of the Barbados Programme of Action in 1994, SIDS have achieved on average positive annual growth rates in their economies. Most SIDS have also recorded human development indices in the medium to high range, reflecting strong, positive performance in important social indicators, particularly literacy and health.

The generally strong economic performance is attributed to the efforts of SIDS at economic diversification, focusing on tourism, the exploration of niche markets for goods and, in some successful cases, such as in the Bahamas, Barbados and Mauritius, development of the financial services sector, particularly off-shore banking services.

Domestic Economy and International Tourism
(International Tourism receipts/ Gross Domestic Product)

Country	Population 2002	GDPpc ($) 1995	GDPpc ($) 2000	GDPpc ($) 2002	ITR/GDP % 1995	ITR/GDP % 2000	ITR/GDP % 2002
Maldives	320,170	1,606	2,167	2,090	52.9	51.4	49.8
Antigua and Barbuda	67,450	7,366	9,915	10,681	50.0	43.6	38.0
Saint Lucia	160,150	3,314	4,077	3,912	47.8	40.4	31.0
Bahamas	295,130	12,566	16,468	16,497	38.4	35.3	34.9
Barbados	276,180	7,284	9,664	9,345	33.6	28.3	26.5
Vanuatu	196,180	1,366	1,200	1,127	25.4	25.2	-
Grenada	89,210	2,994	4,001	4,059	19.6	22.9	22.0
St Vincent & Grenadines	116,390	2,380	3,004	3,219	15.5	22.3	23.0
S. Tome and Principe	170,370	356	317	348	0.0	21.3	18.5
Jamaica	2,680,030	2,136	2,835	2,913	20.3	18.1	15.7
Dominica	70,160	3,056	3,769	3,536	15.5	17.8	18.1
Saint Kitts and Nevis	38,740	5,352	6,714	7,270	28.1	17.6	15.7
Samoa	178,630	1,219	1,387	1,508	17.0	17.3	17.0
Seychelles	80,100	6,748	7,644	8,634	19.3	16.9	18.5
Dominican Republic	8,596,130	1,567	2,381	2,469	13.0	14.4	12.9
Mauritius	1,200,210	3,347	3,729	3,782	11.4	12.3	13.4
Fiji	856,350	2,488	2,032	2,169	14.2	11.0	14.3
Cape Verde	408,760	1,257	1,240	1,428	2.0	7.6	10.2
Comoros	614,380	466	358	402	9.1	7.4	4.6
Bahrain	656,400	10,083	11,545	11,495	4.2	7.2	8.8
Kiribati	96,340	592	570	609	4.3	5.6	-
Tonga	106,140	1,586	1,585	1,348	6.5	4.4	6.6
Papua New Guinea	5,172,030	1,124	676	512	1.3	2.7	0.0
Trinidad and Tobago	1,111,510	4,056	6,499	7,346	1.4	2.6	2.4
Haiti	7,405,260	394	495	429	2.0	1.4	-
Solomon Islands	494,790	928	703	659	4.5	1.2	0.3

Source: WTO based on IMF data (GDP)
GDPpc: Gross Domestic Product per capita
ITR: International Tourism Receipts

For SIDS, international tourism has a very substantial impact on trade levels - on foreign exchange earnings, consumption, the creation of value added and investment, as well as in its contribution to gross domestic product, debt repayment, and job creation.

Notwithstanding the opportunities for economic diversification and growth presented by globalization, nearly all SIDS report high vulnerability in economic performance, including concerns of marginalization in the challenging international economic conditions created as a result of globalization.

Growth in tourism fared well in SIDS. This key economic sector was negatively affected by the impact of international terrorism in 2001, but has begun to show signs of recovery, albeit with increased operating costs for security incurred. The impact of external shocks has shown how vital tourism is as the main contributor to wealth generation in SIDS and how volatile this sector is if not planned and managed properly.

Small islands are by nature insulated and, in many cases, situated in remote places. This makes the access of people and goods difficult and expensive. Infrequency of air service makes the routes to these islands generally expensive.

SIDS have a high degree of dependence on the tourism sector and a high level of leakage from their gross tourism receipts. Some of the tourist-generated revenues leak out of the economy. The leakages are made up primarily of imported goods and services and the repatriation of profits. The extent of these leakages influences the economic benefits received by the local population.

The percentage of imported goods and services in GDP was extremely high in some small island countries such as Seychelles, Antigua and Barbuda, Sao Tome and Principe, and Grenada. This high dependence on imported goods and services can raise the issue of "leakage".

Imports of Goods and Services (% of GDP)

Country	1997	1998	1999
Antigua and Barbuda	84.7	83.5	87.2
Barbados	58.8	56.1	55.4
Cape Verde	55.4	52.3	50.3
Dominica	64.0	60.6	67.2
Dominican Republic	36.2	39.5	38.8
Grenada	66.0	74.6	76.5
Haiti	23.0	29.1	27.7
Jamaica	56.5	54.7	58.6
Madagascar	30.0	29.3	32.7
Mauritius	67.3	68.1	68.9
Sao Tome and Principe	94.0	72.5	84.3
Seychelles	81.4	87.4	88.5
St. Kitts and Nevis	70.9	69.9	69.9

Source: WTO/OMT (based on World Trade Organization data)

Some islands have tourism leakages up to 56%, on account of goods and services required to be imported, repatriation of profits by overseas resort developers/hotel owners, and remittance of funds by expatriate labour.

For some SIDS most of the food produce (vegetables, fruit, meat etc) consumed by tourists and locals has to be imported as the local people have given up growing food. Despite very suitable climatic conditions, food related tourism leakages could be unnecessarily high.

However, for other SIDS tourism has been increasingly utilized as a catalyst for the development of agriculture, fisheries, handicrafts and other services, with locals being encouraged to invest in such projects, to maximize tourism earnings retention.

It should be government policy to aim at maximizing tourism earnings by encouraging local investment in specific areas with a view to satisfy the tourists' needs with locally produced goods and services.

Also, sustainability should be given primary consideration in small island tourism development. The biodiversity and other fragile natural and cultural resources, as well as cleanliness and safety in the destination, can determine the competitiveness of an island nation.

Sustainable tourism must be economically viable and internationally competitive.

Despite their vulnerability, some SIDS have performed particularly well over the last 12 years, for some of them (SIDS members of WTO) the adoption of sustainable tourism development practices has been instrumental in achieving significant growth.

International tourist arrivals at frontiers by country of destination

	1990	1995	(x 1,000) 2000	2001	2002	Accumulated growth 1990-2002	Average annual growth 1990-2002
World	**456,125**	**550,845**	**688,448**	**683,920**	**704,278**	**54.4%**	**3.7%**
SIDS Members of WTO							
Aruba	433	619	721	691	643	48.4%	
Bahrain	1,376	1,396	2,420	2,789	3,167	130.2%	
Cape Verde	24	28	83	115	126	425.0%	
Cuba	327	742	1,741	1,736	1,656	406.4%	
Cyprus	1,561	2,100	2,686	2,697	2,418	54.9%	
Dominican Republic	1,305	1,776	2,972	2,882	2,811	115.4%	
Fiji	279	318	294	348	398	42.7%	
Haiti	144	145	140	142	142	-1.4%	
Jamaica	989	1,147	1,323	1,277	1,266	28.0%	
Maldives	195	315	467	461	485	148.7%	
Malta	872	1,116	1,216	1,180	1,134	30.0%	
Mauritius	292	422	656	660	682	133.6%	
Sao Tome and Principe	3	6	7	8	8	153.3%	
Seychelles	104	121	130	130	132	26.9%	
Total SIDS Members of WTO	**7,904**	**10,251**	**14,856**	**15,116**	**15,067**	**90.6%**	**5.5%**
SIDS not Members of WTO							
Anguilla	31	39	44	48	44	41.9%	
Antigua and Barbuda	206	220	237	222	222	7.8%	
Bahamas	1,562	1,598	1,544	1,538	1,513	-3.1%	
Barbados	432	442	545	507	498	15.3%	
Comoros	8	23	24	19	19	137.5%	
Cook Islands	34	48	73	75	73	114.7%	
Dominica	45	60	70	66	69	53.3%	
Grenada	76	108	129	123	132	73.7%	
Kiribati	3	4	5	5	5	80.0%	
Marshall Islands	5	6	5	5	6	20.0%	
Micronesia (Fed.St.of)	..	..	21	15	19	..	
Niue	1	2	2	1	2	110.0%	
Palau	33	53	58	54	59	78.8%	
Papua New Guinea	41	42	58	54	54	31.7%	
Saint Lucia	141	231	270	250	253	79.4%	
Samoa	48	68	88	88	89	85.4%	
Singapore	4,842	6,422	6,917	6,725	6,997	44.5%	
Solomon Islands	9	12	..	..	..	..	
St.Kitts and Nevis	73	79	73	71	68	-6.8%	
St.Vincent and Grenadines	54	60	73	71	78	44.4%	
Tonga	21	29	35	32	37	76.2%	
Trinidad and Tobago	195	260	399	383	384	96.9%	
Tuvalu	1	1	1	1	1	30.0%	
US.Virgin Islands	463	454	607	592	553	19.4%	
Vanuatu	35	44	57	53	49	41.3%	
Total SIDS not Members of WTO	**8,359**	**10,305**	**11,335**	**10,998**	**11,225**	**34.3%**	**2.5%**

Source: World Tourism Organization

1.3 Measuring the economic impact of tourism

There is no other economic activity that cuts across so many sectors, levels and interests as tourism; and the impacts associated with such inter-dependence can be positive or negative.

Given the dynamism of the industry, there is a vital need to integrate tourism planning with national development and resource management plans, evaluate in advance the costs of tourism development and the likely economic benefits it can bring. For such measurement, governments need an appropriate and proven tool to evaluate the real economic impacts of tourism, namely the Tourism Satellite Accounts (TSA).

The fundamental structure of a TSA is based on the general balance existing within an economy between demand of goods and services generated by tourism and their supply. With the need for strategic planning, policy intervention, the requirements for tourism statistics have expanded considerably over the years. Not only do the Ministries of Tourism have requirements for specialized tourism data needs, but also the same holds true for many interest groups in the industry and the economy.

Within such a generalized perspective TSA information should help to:

- Support strategic planning;
- Assess status and needs of the industry;
- Provide data which makes the system more accountable; and
- Facilitate the management of the tourism industry

Historically, governments and industry associations seeking to promote tourism development have relied on three economic indicators to prove the value of the country's tourism sector:

- Foreign Exchange Generation;
- Employment Creation; and
- Government Revenues.

A standard economic study on the economic impact of tourism traces flows of money from tourist expenditure, first to businesses and government agencies where tourists spend their money and then to:

- Other businesses: supplying goods and services to tourism related businesses;
- Households: earning income by working in tourism or supporting industries;
- Government: through various taxes and charges on tourists, businesses and households.

The total economic impact of tourism is the sum of direct, indirect, and induced effects within a country, archipelago or island. Any of these impacts may be measured as gross output or sales, income, employment, or value added.

- **Direct effects** are production changes associated with the immediate effects of changes in tourist expenditures. For example, an increase in the number of tourists staying overnight in hotels would directly yield increased sales in the hotel industry. The additional hotel sales and associated changes in hotel payments for wages and salaries, taxes, and supplies and services are direct effects of the tourist expenditures.
- **Indirect effects** are the production changes resulting from various rounds of re-spending of the hotel industry's receipts in other backward-linked industries (i.e., industries supplying products and services to hotels). Changes in sales, employments, and income in the linen and catering supply industries, for example, represent indirect effects of changes in hotel sales. Businesses supplying products and services to the linen and catering supply industries represent another

round of indirect effects, eventually linking hotels in varying degrees to many other economic sectors in the country, region or island.

- **Induced effects** are the changes in economic activity resulting from household spending of income earned directly or indirectly as a result of tourist expenditure. For example, hotel, linen supply and catering employees, supported directly or indirectly by tourism, spend their income in the local region for housing, food, transportation, and the usual array of household product and service needs. The sales, income, and employment that result from household spending of added wage, salary, or proprietor's income are induced effects.
- **Final demand** is the term used by econometric models for sales to the final consumers of goods and services. In almost all cases, the final consumers of tourism goods and services are households. Government spending is also considered as final demand. The same methods for estimating impacts of tourist expenditure can be applied to estimate the economic impacts of government spending, for example, to create and maintain a national park or tourist information centre.

By means of indirect and induced effects, changes in tourist spending can impact virtually every sector of the economy to a greater or lesser degree. The magnitude of secondary effects depends on the propensity of businesses and households in the country, region or island to purchase goods and services from local suppliers. Induced effects are particularly noticeable when a large employer in a region closes a business operation. Supporting industries (indirect effects) lose business and the entire local economy suffers due to the reduction in household income within the country, region or island. Retail stores close and leakages of money from the country, region or island increase as consumers go to external sources for more and more goods and services. Similar effects in the opposite direction are observed when there is a significant increase in employment creation and household income brought about by the opening of a new business operation.

1.3.1 Tourism Satellite Account[1] (TSA)

In order to overcome the difficulties inherent in tourism multipliers studies and other methods of measuring the economic impact of tourism, **WTO is encouraging countries to adopt Tourism Satellite Accounts (TSAs) when preparing National Accounts.** The concept for TSAs has only become possible in recent years as tourism statistics have become more reliable and timely throughout the world.

In 1993, the United Nations Statistical Commission adopted a new System of National Accounts (SNA93) and recommended the use of a new reporting concept called Satellite Accounts to expand the analytical capacity of national accounting for selected economic activities, in a flexible manner without overburdening or disrupting the central system.

TSA is a reporting system allowing for the identification of relevant components from the existing national accounts and the reconstruction of them separately to measure the total economic and employment impact of consumer expenditures, capital investment, government revenues and expenditure, foreign trade and business expenditure derived from tourism.

Compared to traditional systems of measuring the economic impact of tourism, the benefits of using and applying satellite accounting to tourism are clear. TSA demands consistency in data, in that it must balance in terms of supply and demand. A Satellite Account builds a database for tourism that is comprehensive, internally consistent and balanced. Thus the data become justifiable and credible.

TSA would provide information on the visitors' demographic indicators, industry profile, and the distribution, costs and utilization of services and programmes, showing trends over time.

1 For more information on the TSA: http://www.world-tourism.org/frameset/frame_statistics.html

WTO started in 1994 the design of the Tourism Satellite Account project with the basic objective of presenting a comprehensive and integrated framework for estimating production, consumption, capital investment, employment and other related variables of tourism activity, designed to share with National Accounts its basic concepts, definitions, classifications, accounting rules and tables, with the main objective of allowing the international comparability of tourism economic impacts. Developing a TSA requires more and different types of information than traditionally used in tourism analysis.

Benefits of using a TSA:

- It reconciles the demand side data with the supply side data within the account, bringing greater coherence to the definition of the industry;
- It uses a recognized accounting system which will bring enhanced credibility to the economic analysis of the industry;
- It uses an accounting framework that can bring other important information into the analysis of tourism, such as data on value added, including tourism's share of GDP, government revenues, employment or financial flows;
- The accounting framework would provide a useful guide to the development of primary data sources.

TSA provides a way to have an overall view of tourism's impact on the economy on an equal footing with all other sectors.

The design of a TSA takes the form of a basic system of concepts, classifications, definitions, tables, and aggregates linked to the standard tables of SNA93 in the functional perspective. This system has been developed to measure tourism impacts in a national economy on an annual basis.

A complete TSA should provide:

- Macroeconomic aggregates to describe the size and the economic importance of tourism, such as Tourism Value Added and Tourism GDP, consistent with similar aggregates for the total economy and for other productive activities and functional areas of interest;
- Detailed data on tourist consumption, and how this consumption is met by domestic supply and imports;
- Detailed production accounts of the tourism related industries including data on employment, linkages with other productive economic activities, and capital formation;
- A link between economic data and other non monetary information on tourism, such as number of arrivals, length of stay, purpose of visit, modes of transport, etc; and
- Basic information required for the development of models of economic impact of tourism (at national and supranational level), for the preparation of tourism market oriented analysis, etc.

For SIDS that have established Tourism Satellite Accounts, like the Dominican Republic since 1994, the TSA has provided the country the necessary tools to develop and plan tourism development to maximize its benefits and to measure its real impact on the economy: top earner among SIDS since the year 2000, international tourism brought the Dominican Republic US$ 2.86 billion, representing 14.4% of the GDP.

Top 15 Earners among SIDS in terms of International Tourism Receipts

Country	International Tourism Receipts (US$ Million)				
	1995	2000	2001	2002	2003
Dominican Republic	1,568	2,860	2,798	2,736	3,110
Cuba	963	1,737	1,692	1,633	-
Bahamas	1,346	1,737	1,650	1,763	1,759
United States Virgin Islands	822	1,206	1,323	1,195	1,271
Jamaica	1,069	1,333	1,233	1,209	1,336
Aruba	521	815	825	832	852
Barbados	612	711	687	648	-
Bahrain	247	573	630	741	-
Mauritius	430	542	624	612	695
Maldives	211	321	327	318	388
Antigua and Barbuda	247	290	272	274	301
Saint Lucia	268	279	233	210	282
Fiji	283	181	217	261	349
Trinidad and Tobago	73	213	201	224	-
Seychelles	98	105	111	129	126

Source: WTO, 2004

1.3.2 Trade in services/ Tourism

International tourism has a very substantial impact on trade levels, as well as on foreign exchange earnings and the balance of payments. Tourism is a significant activity in almost half of the low-income countries as SIDS.

Tourism in Relation to Merchandise Exports

Country	Tourism (%)			Food (%)			Agriculture (%)		
	1990	2000	Growth 90-00	1990	2000	Growth 90-00	1990	2000	Growth 90-00
HAITI	22.3	21.8	22.0	14.0	15.2	14.6	1.2	..	0.5
JAMAICA	39.7	54.1	47.9	19.2	24.0	21.6	..	..	..
MAURITIUS	17.0	26.2	22.4	32.0	24.2	27.6	1.5	..	0.6

Source: WTO

Countries showing deficits in service trade tend to have a small share of international tourism receipts in the service export total: Papua New Guinea (24%), Sri Lanka (26%), Haiti (32%), Iceland (25%), Madagascar (34%) and Cape Verde (27%).

International Trade and Tourism

Countries	BOP Merchandise (US$mn)		BOP Commercial Service (US$mn)		Tourism% Service Export		Tourism% Total Export		Tourism% BOP Merchandise	
	1998	1999	1998	1999	1998	1999	1998	1999	1998	1999
Bahamas	-1,360	-870	578	885	89%	84%	57%	52%	100%	173%
Barbados	-758	-792	586		71%		56%		93%	85%
Cape Verde	-230		-11		27%		24%		9%	
Comoros	-45								36%	
Cuba	-1,940	-2,360	1,814		67%		40%		81%	73%
Dom. Republic	-2,608	-3,000	1,121	1,478	88%	89%	29%	31%	82%	84%
Dominica	-73	-87	27		53%		28%		52%	56%
Fiji	-71		155		51%		22%		344%	
Haiti	-622	-829	-192		32%		16%		9%	
Jamaica	-1,685	-1,456	494	531	69%	71%	39%	44%	71%	88%
Madagascar	-271		-62		34%		18%		34%	
Maldives	-278	-338	230		93%		75%		109%	96%
Mauritius	-373	-592	205		55%	51%	19%	21%	135%	92%
Papua New Guinea	543	689	-476		24%	31%	4%	4%	14%	11%
Samoa	-81		29		66%		52%		47%	
Seychelles	-338		137		42%		34%		33%	
Solomon Islands	-29		-2		13%		4%		24%	
Sri Lanka	-1,092	-1,294	-437		26%		4%		21%	21%
Trinidad and Tobago	-748	-230	339		35%		7%		27%	
Vanuatu	-54		69		47%		36%		96%	

Source: WTO based on World Trade Organization data
BOP: Balance of Payments

Many small island countries are highly dependent on international tourism. In the case of Maldives, international tourism receipts accounted for 93% of its commercial service export total and 75% of total exports from the country. The situation is similar in Aruba, the Bahamas, and Dominican Republic.

In many countries, international tourism receipts pay off the trade deficit caused by merchandise imports. International tourism brings Fiji, the Bahamas, Maldives, Mauritius, Jamaica, Barbados, and Dominican Republic sufficient or nearly sufficient foreign exchange to cover merchandise trade deficits.

Despite the importance of tourism in the world economy, many have criticized the manner in which tourism has been dealt within the framework of the General Agreement on Trade in Services (GATS).

The World Tourism Organization is working currently to revise this unsatisfactory classification in the current negotiations on trade in services. The basic argument is that the current definitions of tourism in the GATS is wrongly based on the assumption that tourism produces and supplies homogenous products or services like traditional industries, while instead it is a collection of products and services, ranging from airlines to catering, to entertainment and many others. This view is also stressed by the TSA, breaking down visitor's expenditures to analyse the direct and indirect effects of tourism in terms of generation value - added, employment, personal income and government revenue.

It is important to underline at this point that tourism expenditures have a flow through, or catalytic effect on, the economy in terms of production as well as employment. This process originates a demand for local supplies of consumer and intermediate goods, depending on the level of economic development and capital equipments. The supply of such goods can stimulate the development of small businesses as well as create links with the informal sector. These links are not automatic but have to be enhanced.

Another crucial area is the institutional framework in which tourism investors operate, whether foreign or domestic. They will be attracted to invest in the tourism industry in a specific country or destination only if the macro economic framework is conducive to the private sector investments. Macro-economic policies that create such an enabling environment should foster stability, confidence and predictability.

Chapter 2

Tourism, a less disruptive development option for SIDS

2.1 Tourism, one of the most successful nature based industries

"Meeting the needs of human society without destroying the living earth that sustains us all is a huge challenge. We depend on natural resources for food, water, energy and many other materials that are the physical basis of our cultures and civilization. Yet we also value the natural world around us for its own sake, for recreation and as an important part of our heritage. Natural systems are the fruit of many complex processes and their often-delicate balances are easily disturbed by thoughtless human action. We have a duty to preserve them for those who will come after us."

Gisbert Glaser, UNEP

Many small island countries are economically underdeveloped with few economic development options, but have outstanding cultural and natural resources suitable for tourism. In the last decade, most SIDS have long recognized the importance of sustainable tourism for their environments and peoples. The tourism share in islands' GDP has increased against manufacturing and agriculture in many island destinations.

The general pattern discerned in SIDS is that smaller states tend to be relatively more dependant on tourism then larger entities. Among other factors, this is the result of limited resource endowments that have historically hindered the formation of a diversified economic base. Hence, tourism contributions to Gross Domestic Product in the magnitude of 20-50% are common among smaller island states.

However, the vast majority of SIDS are facing severe challenges in finding ways to sustain their economies because they find it almost impossible to make their agricultural and manufacturing sector internationally competitive.

The ongoing difficulties in SIDS economies result from a combination of factors that include:

- **Loss of market and declining value of traditional exports:** as a result of the new World Trade Organization (WTO/OMC) rules, non-LDCs (least developed countries) SIDS have experienced the loss of preferential access for their exports to developed countries' markets. It has also forced SIDS to selling commodities at declining prices without the benefits of economy of scale, with very high transportation costs due to geographic isolation and small freight volumes. All this has resulted in significantly reduced export earnings. Preferential access to these markets that paid prices significantly higher than world prices based on historical relationships, were associated with the colonial history of the SIDS and these developed countries. Caribbean SIDS provide a very good example of this. Between 1995, the first year of the WTO/OMC, and 2000, the unit value of 7 of the 11 most important exports fell. For 5 of these exports (coffee, sugar, etc.), the decline was greater than 25%. Consequently, the trade deficit increased from US$1.2 billion in 1994 to US$3.4 billion (almost triple) in 2001.
- **Declining domestic food production and increasing imports:** The World Trade Organization requirement for reduced tariffs on imports, along with overproduction of agricultural products for export in developed countries, is negatively affecting food production in SIDS. Local farmers cannot compete with the price of imported products, subsequently, they have to either stop or

significantly reduce production. Therefore, SIDS are experiencing increasing levels of food imports. In Caribbean SIDS, the cost of food imports increased by 47% between 1994 and 2001.

As a consequence of these and other developments, including reduction in tourism caused by the terrorist attacks on the USA in September 2001, SIDS are experiencing increasing external debt, and limited economic growth; the exception are some SIDS, such as Cape Verde and Samoa, because of their Least Developed Country (LDCs) status, thereby enjoying preferential treatment.

In adopting sustainable tourism policies, tourism can leave more foreign exchange in the country than most other economic sectors, in absolute as well as in relative figures. A GTZ study conducted in Latin America and the Caribbean showed that if an all-inclusive trip costs US$ 1,000, approximately US$ 300 of this sum are spent on the services in the host country. Even if the hotel's operating authority is an international chain that re-exports US$ 100 of it as profit, US$ 200 or 20% of the final retail price remain in the country, shared out between wages, other services, purchases of goods in the local economy (e.g. a medium-sized all-inclusive facility (3-500 rooms) purchases fish and meat for approximately US$ 250,000-400,000 on average per year in the country. Resorts surveyed obtain 70-90% of all agricultural products from national production; goods are only imported if the country cannot produce them in the required quantity and quality). The local net product of course increases if the hotel chain is a local enterprise.

For most SIDS, leakages in agriculture and manufacturing can be much higher than leakages in tourism. For instance, from a consumption of coffee for US$ 1,000 in Germany, only US$ 140 reach the country of origin, of which US$ 100 or 10% at best end up in the coffee farmer pocket. Even if the selling price is increased with Fair Trade practices by 20 or 30%, the return to the farmer comes to 12 or 13% of the final retail price.

With regard to the environmental issues, where agriculture is the dominant economic activity, soil quality and freshwater resources will determine its present and future productivity. Where tourism and fisheries are the major industries, the states must use their marine and coastal environments intensively. It is therefore clear that further tourism, agricultural or fisheries development without the necessary environmental safeguards will be destabilizing. Without mentioning again the indiscriminate trade liberalization that is threatening the future of the main source of exports of crops, such as sugar, banana and fisheries.

In many islands of the Caribbean for example, with the decline of the export oriented sugar cane industry, the traditional hospitality of the people was institutionalized and transformed into a tourism industry.

In the islands of the Indian Ocean and the Pacific tourism has been developed more recently and in many of these countries is now a major economic activity, providing much needed foreign currency, income, and employment to the people. In the Pacific, of the 20 states comprising over 1,650 islands, 14 states identified tourism as the main source for future income (Bank of Hawaii, 2001).

However, the extent of tourism benefits that a community can harvest would vary from country to country, depending on the structure of the economy, availability of tourism inputs, institutional strength, and government policy on tourism. Many island countries have experienced booms and slumps in tourism, caused due to both external and internal factors, but the extent of dependence on tourism determines the magnitude of its impacts to the people.

Hence, proper tourism management, to ensure sustainability and to maximize the benefits to the local economy has become very important.

Tourism offers one of the few opportunities for economic diversification in small islands. It has many linkages with other economic sectors, and if integrated into national development plans with adequate provisions for intersectoral linkages, it can contribute to the growth of tourism-related activities in all of the major economic sectors - agriculture, including fishing, industry and services, including transportation. Many small island developing states have established initiatives to balance tourism activities with broader economic, social and environmental objectives at the regional, national and local levels. In particular, major efforts have led to:

- The strengthening of regional cooperation on strategies, standards and capacity-building for tourism, with the assistance of international institutions, the private sector and nongovernmental organizations in the area of human and institutional capacity-building;
- Increased use of user charges, particularly for environmental protection;
- Formulation of integrated national action plans, strategies and policies which include tourism, in particular its environmental aspects;
- The establishment of frameworks that allow local communities to participate and have greater control over tourism development in their localities.

Tourism is in a special position to address critical issues of sustainable development, achieving the right balance between social, economic and environmental goals. Because of its high dependence on many other support activities, it is an industry around which the three dimensions of sustainability can be strongly inter-related:

- **Socially**, in providing jobs to a large proportion of the population, including women and unskilled labour force, tourism contributes to the respect of human rights and equal opportunities for all in society. It requires an equitable distribution of benefits, with a focus on eradicating poverty: emphasis on local communities to maintain and strengthen their life support systems, recognizing and respecting different cultures and avoiding any form of exploitation.
- **Economically**, in the generation of prosperity and the efficiency and effectiveness of all economic activity. As a major foreign exchange generator, tourism is vital for island nations if a right balance is maintained between tourism revenues and leakages. Its multiplier effect represents a powerful development option for island economies.
- **Environmentally**, in the conservation and management of resources, especially those which are non renewable or are precious in terms of life support. It includes concern for minimizing pollution of air, land and water, and its consequences, and the conservation of biological diversity and natural heritage.

Taking into account environmental, social and economic aspects is key to guaranteeing the long term survival of tourism as well as conserving the environment. Sustainable tourism can be a major industry for generating income and protecting the environment, especially in areas important for their biological diversity and natural beauty.

2.2 How to reinforce positive and mitigate negative tourism impacts

2.2.1 The global context in sustainability and tourism

The increasing pressures for accelerated economic development on the one hand, and international environmental issues on the other makes it a very difficult challenge to integrate economic development and environmental protection, as guided by Agenda 21 and the Barbados Program of Action. Considering their vulnerability, SIDS have to establish an appropriate institutional framework to adopt fundamental principles and processes that should lead to a greater capacity to understand, monitor and cope with emerging environmental issues, all of which call for a greater and wider involvement of all stakeholders.

The Barbados Programme of Action in 1994 set forth specific actions and measures to be taken at the national, regional and international levels in support of the sustainable development of SIDS; it included:

1994 Barbados Plan of Action for the Sustainable Development of SIDS

I.	Preamble
II.	Climate change and sea level rise
III.	Natural and environmental disasters
IV.	Management of waste
V.	Coastal and marine resources
VI.	Freshwater resources
VII.	Land resources
VIII.	Energy resources
IX.	**Tourism resources**
X.	Biodiversity resources
XI.	National institutions and administrative capacity
XII.	Regional institutions and technical cooperation
XIII.	Transport and communication
XIV.	Science and technology
XV.	Human resource development
XVI.	Implementation, monitoring and review

Although tourism appears as a sector on its own, because of its complexity, tourism impacts and opportunities would need to be fully integrated in most of the other sectors defined; indeed, tourism has obvious links with coastal and marine resources, biodiversity resources, freshwater resources, land resources, energy resources, management of waste, transport and communication and human resource development, while institutional and implementation aspects are also relevant in tourism.

As much as local impacts can be addressed and mitigated through existing guidelines and policies on a national and regional level, the external impacts as climate change and sea level rise, natural and environmental disasters need a consolidated approach with the international community and assistance from agencies specialized in this field.

Ever since the leading international fora decided it was necessary to lay down a new groundwork for addressing the viability of development, a series of key criteria and concepts concerning the interrelationship between tourism, the environment, and sustainability have been formulated, in turn necessitating the reformulation of many parameters and new procedures in use today.

It is recognized that several active international and regional networks of SIDS exist over the globe, working on areas of concern within the BPOA, and more specifically for environmental sustainability; but it is only recently that tourism has been taken into consideration in the various national and regional programs carried out.

The Ministries of Tourism of Small island nations should work closely and create synergies within their territory with all stakeholders involved in sustainability issues, essentially with institutions such as Ministries of Environment, Culture, Land Use, Energy, with NGO and the private sector, to make the optimum use of existing programs that could benefit tourism development and management, as well as to sensitize all stakeholders on the importance of tourism, to be adequately planned and integrated in future programs.

During the World Summit on Sustainable Development in 2002, the Johannesburg Plan of Implementation (JPoI) calls for undertaking a full and comprehensive review of the implementation of the BPOA considering the specificities of SIDS and tourism. Therefore, the final Plan of Implementation, agreed by Heads of State at Johannesburg, includes a specific paragraph (43) concerning Tourism. Four more paragraphs make reference to tourism, of which the one on energy (20) and the one on Small Island Developing States (58).

About Small Island Developing States (58), the Johannesburg Plan of Implementation recommends to *"develop community-based initiatives on sustainable tourism by 2004, and build the capacities necessary to diversify tourism products, while protecting culture and traditions, and effectively conserving and managing natural resources."*

World Summit on Sustainable Development
Extract of the Plan of Implementation (paragraph 43)
Johannesburg, South Africa, 26 August - 4 September 2002

43. Promote sustainable tourism development, including non consumptive tourism and ecotourism, taking into account the spirit of the International Year of Eco-tourism 2002, the United Nations Year for Cultural Heritage in 2002, the World Eco-tourism Summit 2002 and its Quebec Declaration, and the **Global Code of Ethics for Tourism as adopted by the World Tourism Organization**, in order to increase the benefits from tourism resources for the population in host communities while maintaining the cultural and environmental integrity of the host communities and enhancing the protection of ecologically sensitive areas and natural heritages.

Promote sustainable tourism development and capacity-building in order to contribute to the strengthening of rural and local communities.

This would include actions at all levels to:

(a) Enhance international cooperation, foreign direct investment and partnerships with both private and public sectors, at all levels;

(b) Develop programmes, including education and training programmes, that encourage people to participate in ecotourism, enable indigenous and local communities to develop and benefit from ecotourism, and enhance stakeholder cooperation in tourism development and heritage preservation, in order to improve the protection of the environment, natural resources and cultural heritage;

(c) Provide technical assistance to developing countries and countries with economies in transition to support sustainable tourism business development and investment and tourism awareness programmes, to improve domestic tourism, and to stimulate entrepreneurial development;

(d) Assist host communities in managing visits to their tourism attractions for their maximum benefit, while ensuring the least negative impacts on and risks for their traditions, culture and environment, with the support of the World Tourism Organization and other relevant organizations;

(e) Promote the diversification of economic activities, including through the facilitation of access to markets and commercial information, and participation of emerging local enterprises, especially small and medium-sized enterprises.

There is a need for tourism stakeholders at all levels, be they public or private, **to work closely with those responsible for nature conservation. Their joint cooperation should ensure** that the twin objectives of conservation and development are suitably balanced and **that tourism effectively contributes to safeguard the planet's precious resources.**

Seychelles Environment Management Plan (EMPS) 2000-2010: Integration of sustainable policies in all sectors and tourism

The example of Seychelles is relevant in its capacity to create a coordinated approach between all related sectors of the country for sustainable development. Tourism in the Seychelles is seen to be instrumental to conserve biodiversity because managed in a sustainable manner.

To achieve this very ambitious and challenging vision, the country has put in place planning mechanisms and modern policies elaborated in close consultation and collaboration with the Civil Society, Private Sector and NGO's, like VISION 21, a comprehensive master plan for sustainable tourism development in Seychelles released in 2001. This nation of only 80,000 people has created the appropriate environment to responsibly plan, control and limit the development of its tourism industry so guaranteeing that it will minimize the impact on the sustainability of its unique ecosystems.

Identified as one of the 24 hotspots of biodiversity on the planet, Seychelles has a strong history of conservation and environment activities, which has been heightened over the last 12 years through the development and implementation of environmental management plans. The country is currently implementing its second Environment Management Plan 2000-2010.

The overall goal of the EMPS 2000 - 2010 is to promote, coordinate and integrate sustainable development programmes that cut across all sectors of society in the Seychelles, including tourism.

"At the dawn of the 21st century it is the vision of the people of Seychelles that this second generation EMPS 2000 - 2010, will serve as a flexible, yet robust, vehicle for continued improvement of proactive environmental management excellence, so that by the year 2010 the Seychelles will be firmly established globally as a committed leader in sustainable development."
The overall goal of the EMPS 2000 - 2010 is the promotion, coordination and integration of sustainable development programmes that cut across all sectors of society in the Seychelles in order to attain the above mission.

Ten thematic areas were chosen to cover all major social and economic sectors as well as certain key subjects of relevance to environmental management such as environmental economics. Other cross-sectoral themes that would cut across the main thematic areas were also identified.

- Society, Population and Health (including Gender)
- Land Use, Coastal Zones and Urbanization Biodiversity,
- Forestry and Agriculture
- Energy and Transport
- Fisheries and Marine Resources/Processes
- Water, Sanitation and Waste
- Tourism and Aesthetics
- Environmental Economics,
- Mainstreaming and Sustainable Financing Regulatory,

- Policy and Institutional Mechanisms Commerce,
- Industry and Production

This vision and overall goal will be pursued through a strategy that integrates core principles. Widely embodied in Agenda 21. These principles will guide all of the programmes that form part of the EMPS 2000 - 2010.

These principles are also embedded in the Seychelles Constitution and guided by the sustainable principles stated in the EMPS 2000 - 2010. The Seychelles Constitution provides under Article 38, the right to every person to live in and enjoy a clean, healthy and ecologically balanced environment in Seychelles.

Source: Environment Management Plan of Seychelles 2000-2010

2.2.2 Tourism, a driving force in the conservation and protection of nature and culture

The concept of environmental quality is constantly expanding and is becoming an unavoidable precondition for the competitiveness of all tourism destinations. Tourism is one of the target sectors for environmental policies, and consumers, the tourists, are constantly raising the level of their demands and expectations in this respect.

It is no longer merely a question of scenery. Today, demands for environmental quality extend to basic issues relating to the conservation of ecosystems and biodiversity, consumption of resources (water, energy, materials, etc.), waste treatment, atmospheric emissions, and so on.

Islands are generally more vulnerable environments than continental areas and this is so for various reasons:

- With some notable exceptions, islands are small territories with reduced biodiversity and closer interdependence among its natural components. This means that negative impacts impinged upon one of the elements are easily and quickly felt throughout the entire island.
- Islands generally have limited fresh water resources and are, therefore, dependent on external and normally expensive sources, or on an adequate use and conservation of their natural sources.
- Islands are much more sensitive than continents to sea level rises resulting from climate change.
- Because of their size, waste disposal in islands presents additional environmental difficulties than those normally found in bigger, continental territories.
- Islands have smaller populations and these usually share a fairly unique history and culture that can be easily affected by external influences.
- Most of small island developing states are heavily dependent on tourism for their foreign exchange earnings, employment opportunities and in many cases the generation of GDP.

If tourism is not well planned, developed and managed, it can generate several types of negative environmental impacts, such as:

- **Water pollution** resulting from improper waste management of sewage and solid waste systems of hotels and other tourist facilities. Water pollution includes pollution of river, lake and coastal waters from sewage outfall lines and of ground water by seepage of waste materials.
- **Air pollution** resulting from excessive use of internal combustion vehicles, fossil fuel for energy generation. Aircraft generate some air pollution.
- **Noise pollution** resulting from tourist activities and tourist vehicles including aircraft movements.
- Vehicular and pedestrian **traffic congestion** generated by tourists at popular attraction and facility sites.
- **Unattractive landscapes** (visual pollution) resulting from several factors: poor design of hotels and other tourist facilities; badly planned layout of facilities (poor land use and site planning); inadequate landscaping of tourist facilities; use of large and ugly advertising signs; and obstruction of scenic views by tourism development.
- **Littering** of the landscape by tourists and defacing of features by graffiti and vandalism.
- **Ecological disruption** of natural areas and disturbance of wildlife by overuse and misuse by tourists and inappropriate tourism development.
- **Coastal and marine environments** in small islands are all important types of tourism areas and are particularly vulnerable to ecological damage. In coastal areas, for example, onshore development may increase erosion and runoff with sedimentation into the coastal waters which smother and kill coral reefs.
- **Damage to archaeological and historic sites** by inappropriate tourism development, and due to overuse and misuse by tourists.
- **Environmental hazards** such as erosion, land slippage, damage from high waves, flooding, earthquakes etc. and land use problems resulting from poor planning, sitting and engineering of tourist facilities,

Measures for coping with environmental impacts would imply:

- the development of a multidisciplinary approach for rigorous vetting of tourism development proposals, taking into account prospective cumulative impacts of tourism development, and establishment of environmental standards for approval of projects.
- appropriate review and revision of existing taxes and subsidies to ensure that they are in fact conducive to sustainable development, and development of additional economic instruments to better internalise environmental costs;
- imposition of appropriate user fees for the use of national terrestrial land marine or parks and reserves, and earmarking the accrued receipts for purposes of improvement and management of sensitive areas;
- inducing the tourism industry, through appropriate user charges, to meet the full cost of freshwater that it uses, and to contribute adequately to solid waste management and cleaning of beaches;
- implementing a sustainable marketing strategy in cooperation with all partners involved in the tourism industry; and encouraging voluntary initiatives and adherence to codes of conduct by the business community and visitors.

Tourism development must be monitored by introducing adaptation and mitigation measures to ensure that no serious negative impacts are taking place, as well as appropriate policies, involving all tourism stakeholders. One of the techniques recommended is to monitor impacts by using sustainability indicators: economic, social and environmental indicators are developed in chapter IV of this publication. Indicators need to be periodically measured and if problems are emerging, corrective action should be taken. The quality of the tourism product must be maintained and the product periodically revitalized so that tourist satisfaction levels remain at a high level and the tourist markets are retained.

The guiding principle for sustainable tourism development is to manage the natural and human resources so as to maximize visitor enjoyment and local benefit while minimizing negative impacts upon the destination site, community and local population.

This requires an objective assessment of potential negative impacts and a thoughtful analysis of how this potential can be controlled. In identifying tourism development factors and their negative impacts, mitigating or corrective actions can be defined and applied. Corrective actions are based upon the assumption that the negative impact has already occurred. Better advance planning would obviously be more desirable, in order to prevent the occurrence of negative impacts.

In Malta for example, initiatives have been taken by the government to ease the ever growing concerns related to waste. Since a few years ago, the Malta Hotels and Restaurants Association (MHRA) has encouraged hoteliers and practitioners to proactively develop new strategies concerning Professional eco management. Concerned about the importance of the overall quality of the tourism product in Malta, MHRA issued a 50-page Green Hotel Guide, a practical guide for members to use so as to be able to work in a greener and more environmentally sustainable way. However, a recent eco tax bill which was passed through Parliament has caused some commotion among the business community.

Malta: Eco Contribution Act of 2004

The bill which is cited as the Eco Contribution Act of 2004 is designed to try and solve part of the problems and issues related to waste disposal on the island. Over the past decade a number of initiatives have been taken by the government to ease the ever growing concerns related to waste. During the first eight months of 2003, for example, the largest landfill site on the island, received over 685 thousand tones of waste: 77% was related to debris material taken from building sites and development zones while 15% came from municipal waste.

On the smaller island of Gozo, the picture was pretty similar with the exception that there was a larger percentage of municipal/trade debris collected. The reasons for this pointed to the fact that Gozo enjoys an internal as well as external tourism market and there are a number of hotels and outlets which cater for the visitor.

Various studies have shown that the waste problem in Malta and Gozo could get worse because of two primary factors: the general lifestyle and culture as well as the depletion of possible zones for developing landfills.

Ironically, tourism, which is the largest socio-economic activity on the island, could be threatened if drastic action is not taken now. Last year a row blew up about the use of engineered landfills as a possible solution to waste disposal and now the Government wants to tackle the problem at its very source – by curbing all environmentally unsafe materials.

The eco contribution will be paid at the time the items are put on the market and, as an incentive, those items which are "recovered" are eligible for a credit of the contribution. The bill is based on the concept of "Polluter Pays" and is, obviously designed to get people think about what and how they purchase.

2.2.3 Tourism in Coastal areas

Fragile oasis in the ocean, small islands are bound by the sea on all sides; they appear as self contained systems. It is a misleading perception, as islands interact closely with the water that surround them, as well as with adjacent islands and continental land areas. Small islands have tourism attractions such as sandy beaches, pristine shorelines as well as attractive cultural assets. Many can combine their beach attractions with hills and mountains and unique forms of flora and fauna, not to mention breathtaking underwater coral reefs and marine life.

Any form of life and development is intrinsically linked to impacts on the costal areas and oceans surrounding. Tourism development in SIDS is based of the attractiveness of those idealistic waters and shores, and has been longstanding based on development of those sensitive areas; therefore, special attention has to be addressed to environmental impacts of unsustainable development on costal zones, some of which are highlighted below.

Potential Environmental Impacts of Tourism in Coastal Areas

Potential Impacts	Tourism Development Causes
Coral Reefs and Seagrass	
• Physical damage to coral reefs and collection of organisms	Reef walking, collection of shells & coral, boat anchoring, diving
• Increase in freshwater runoff & sediments	Land clearing for construction
• Introduction of waterborne pollutants (nutrients & pesticides)	Waste water outfalls of poorly treated sewage in coastal waters
Estuaries/lagoons	
• Encroachment	Land filling for siting of structures
• Changes in sedimentation patterns	Placement of structures on beaches and over water
• Changes to the salinity regime	Fresh water runoff
• Introduction of waterborne pollutants	
• Destruction of submerged and fringing vegetation	Runoff, sedimentation, recreational use
• Inlet modifications	Harbour maintenance, siting of buildings and structures
• Loss of fishery habitat increased	Land use modifications, runoff, sedimentation, pollution
Mangroves	
• Changes in freshwater runoff, salinity regime and tidal flow patterns	
• Excessive silting	Construction, sewage discharge
• Introduction of pollutants	
• Conversion of mangrove habitat & over harvesting of resources	Used as a tourism development site
Salt Marshes (tidal flats)	
• Degradation of bird habitat & seed collection	Discharging wastes, fish sites alternation of site for tourism
• Obstruction of storm-water runoff	Alteration of tidal flats for tourism development
Barrier Beaches, Sand Dunes & Spits	
• Sand mining	For construction purposes
• Erosion	Improper sitting of structures
• Dune migration	Removal of natural vegetation

Source: Guide for Local Authorities on Developing Sustainable Tourism/, WTO, 1998

In 2001 during the WTO General Assembly in Japan, his Excellency the President of the Republic of Maldives, Mr. Maumoon Abdul Gayoom, addressed with wisdom the special case of the vulnerability of SIDS:

> "Evolution teaches us an important lesson; that survival requires adaptation. It has been forcefully argued that what had been most important for the survival of species was neither strength nor intelligence, but responsiveness to change.
>
> How willing are we to sustain the earth that nourishes us?
>
> It is now nearly ten years since the historic Earth Summit. Addressing environmental challenges requires the world to act as one. In this critical process, tourism has no doubt a key role to play. This is the age of the people. Tourism is one of the most popular ways the people of the world see and enjoy the world. It demands a living planet, one that is healthy, safe and enjoyable.
>
> To best understand our affinity with conservation, one needs only to think about the unique geography of our archipelago. The Maldives consist of around 1,190 coral islands in 26 natural atolls. All the islands are low-lying. In fact most of the islands do not have a single point over two meters from the mean see level. A rise in the sea-level by one meter could very well drown a whole nation."

The Maldives recognize the importance of developing tourism on a sustainable basis. The development of the tourism industry is carefully planned and managed. Sustainability is the linchpin of the current second ten year master plan, as was the case with its predecessor. In the context of the conservation of marine biodiversity, the following example in Maldives shows how tourism can contribute to protecting the marine life.

Republic of Maldives:
A successful example of protection through the prohibition of activities

In 1992, a survey by the Government of the Maldives found that over US$ 2 million was spent per year by divers who came to watch sharks. It was estimated that reef sharks are about 100 times more able to generate revenue if they are the basis of dive operations, than if they are the basis of a shark fishery. Thus there was a sound economic case for protecting reef sharks, at least within the tourism zones (25 selected sites).

In these areas, prohibited activities included: anchoring (except in an emergency), coral and sand mining, rubbish dumping, removal of any living and non-living resources, and fishing of any kind. Objectives were to protect important dive sites, conserve biodiversity and sustainable development of tourism.

Tourist divers were used to keep track of people breaking the law deliberately or through ignorance. They report their findings. This has created awareness among locals of the importance of many values. As a result, there has been no illegal mining or garbage dumping. However, there is still a need to restrain some visitor practices, such as casual boat anchoring.

The lessons from this project are that marine life can be preserved and protected through regulations, but increasing public awareness is an essential part of this strategy.

Source: WTO, 2001

2.2.4 Tourism in protected areas

As a market-based alternative catering to the growing number of discriminating travellers trying to find, understand and enjoy a natural environment, tourism in protected marine and land areas can also help their sustainable management. Tourism can support the protection of natural resources, as local residents realize the value of their asset and want to preserve it. The link between protected areas and tourism is as old as the history of protected areas. Protected areas need tourism, and tourism needs protected areas. Though the relationship is complex and sometimes adversarial, tourism is always a critical component to consider in the establishment and management of protected areas. The underlying aim is to ensure that tourism contributes to the purposes of protected areas and does not undermine them.

If protected areas are established primarily to preserve some type of biophysical process or condition such as a wildlife population, habitat, natural landscape, or cultural heritage such as a community's cultural tradition, tourists visit these protected areas to understand and appreciate the values for which the area was established and to gain personal benefits.

Tourism planning and development aims to take advantage of the interest shown by tourists so as to:

- enhance economic opportunities,
- protect the natural and cultural heritage, and
- advance the quality of life of all concerned by increasing jobs for local residents

It is worth noting that the number of protected areas worldwide has doubled in the last 12 years, showing the importance and value that such areas represent for a country. For SIDS, new terrestrial and marine protected areas have been instrumental in both conservation and tourism opportunities, as well as responding to a growing demand for ecotourism, nature tourism and community tourism, diving and yachting.

World total protected areas

Years	World total protected areas (number)	Surface area
1992	48,388	12.3 million km2
2003	102,102	18.8 million km2

Source IUCN, World Park Congress 2003

As part of protected areas, **World Heritage Sites** have always been among the main magnets of travel. The masterworks of man and nature prompt in us a sense of wonder that is in itself a supreme form of transportation. But uncontrolled tourism and ill-planned development can cause irreversible physical and social damage, not only to such sites but also to the communities surrounding them.

By bringing together the conservation of cultural and natural heritage under a single legal instrument, the *World Heritage Convention* pioneered some of the thinking which during the 1970's and 1980's evolved to become the core of the concept of sustainable development. The World Heritage Convention seeks to protect natural and cultural properties of "outstanding universal value" against the increasing threat of damage in a rapidly developing world.

The continuously growing tourism industry represents both a threat and a possibility to the future preservation of World Heritage Sites, and strategies for their balanced and harmonious tourism development are required.

Tourism based on protected areas can be a key factor in supporting the conservation of the natural and cultural heritage. It can generate the funds through entrance and service fees, local taxes and in many other ways that can be used directly to help meet or offset the costs of conservation, maintaining cultural traditions and providing education. Indirectly, by demonstrating the economic value that protected area tourism can bring to a country or a region, it can build public and political support for conservation of natural heritage.

Indeed, protected areas can be the engines of sustainable rural development. IUCN advises that protected areas should be repositioned "in the context of community development and the local economy" (IUCN, 1999). It argues that protected areas, sustained by tourist income, not only create jobs and raise income but can also be used to support local communities' needs for:

- **Improved infrastructure**: upgrading roads for tourism access gives neighbouring villages better access to the outside world. Telecommunications access to protected area offices can be vital to local communities in times of emergency;
- **Education**: some protected areas provide language, literacy training to their staff, skills than can then be applied in the community as well;
- **Training**: the training that parks staff receive in such matters as vehicle maintenance or food hygiene will be of practical use in local communities;
- **Health care**: the medical services available to parks staff and visitors can be shared with local communities (IUCN, 1999).

Thus, tourism in terrestrial and marine protected areas may be viewed as a tool to help communities to maintain, or improve, their living standards and quality of life. Even if not an island state, the example of Costa Rica remains one of the most interesting regarding ecotourism, especially in the use of protected areas.

Costa Rica

An example of protected areas creating the foundation of a successful ecotourism industry

Costa Rica's national parks, wildlife refuges and biological reserves cover over 630,000ha, or more than 25% of the country. Much of the land was purchased and operated by government during the 1970s, but there was an economic crisis in the 1980s, and a reduction of international donations in the 1990s. Costa Rica chose to raise national park entrance fees. In addition, a two-tiered fee system was developed so foreigners paid more than residents.

Despite the increased charges, Costa Rica's parks remain a popular international tourist destination. The country had 1.03 million international arrivals in 1999, and – if the 1996 figures are a guide – **66% of those tourists visited a protected area**. Annual tourism receipts in Costa Rica now total over US$ 1 billion, and it is the national park system which forms the foundation for its successful ecotourism industry.

Source: Honey cited in Brown, 2001

Costa Rica
An example of environmental education shaping national values

Environmental education may assist a protected area system in shaping national valuation of natural heritage and conservation. In Costa Rica, for example, when the national park and wildlife reserve system started in the 1960s, there was a low public level of understanding of the need for natural heritage conservation. Thus it was first necessary to develop public understanding and appreciation of the country's exceptional biodiversity. This was accomplished in several ways:

- Encouraging park visitation by residents (valuing through experience); Channelled entry to education facilities in prominent national parks (e.g. via construction of an interpretive visitor centre at the entrance to Volcan Poas National Park);
- Interpretation on site (understanding acquired through displays, materials and interpreters);
- A national school environmental education programme (ensuring future generations understood the country's natural heritage); and
- Encouraging school visits (individual parks introduced active schools programmes).

A biological research industry emerged, as did a major ecotourism industry, both in the private sector. Both led to increased employment for those with education. Over time, ecotourism development fostered local economic development, together with a strong national appreciation of the importance of the natural resources of the country. Through park visitation, environmental education and private ecotourism development, the national parks and the wildlife reserves are now seen as a fundamental feature of Costa Rican society.

Source: Eagles and Higgins, 1998

2.2.5 Enhancing quality of life in the host community

Tourism development should be designed to protect what is good about a host community and tackle those aspects that need to be improved. One way in which this can be achieved is to develop facilities and services for tourism, which can also benefit the living conditions of local residents.

Socially, one of the most immediate benefits of the tourism industry is its ability to create employment and, in the case of tourism, an added benefit is that it caters for both skilled and unskilled employment. As a labour-intensive industry, tourism has the potential to create more jobs per unit of investment than any other industry and tourism can be a useful source of employment.

Tourism, when properly developed and managed, can serve as a mechanism for stimulating the practice of local cultures, folklore, traditions, arts and crafts, and cuisine, protecting natural environments, preserving historical, archaeological and religious monuments.

Tourism can have a profound impact on the economy, society and environment of island nations, as Tourism is a peoples' industry where people are the essence of the tourism activity. People constitute the market, require services from other people and generate the social, cultural and economic interactions which have made tourism such an important activity. Therefore tourism is frequently the leader in bringing infrastructure and social facilities to local people.

The Jamaican Experience

Jamaica is an excellent example that illustrates how tourism can improve the life of local people. The country has had a long and interesting history in tourism. The industry's potential was recognized as long ago as the late nineteenth century when entrepreneurs felt that much profit could be made from promoting Jamaica as a place for rejuvenation and recuperation. With a population of about 2.6 million people, who are descendants of Africans, Chinese, Europeans, east Indians and other racial groups, Jamaicans are heirs to a rich history and heritage, as most island nations. Jamaica has therefore developed a cultural diversity that finds expression in an incredible creativity.

The island's resources support a wide range of primary economic activities including agriculture, bauxite (the raw material of aluminium) and tourism, as well as a number of other enterprises such as fishing, manufacturing and crafts. **It is tourism, however, that is seen as the engine of growth for the country's economy,** contributing some 13% (2001) to the gross domestic product and being the country's largest foreign exchange earner as well as the largest employer of labour.

Though impressive, the national tourism figures do not adequately express the benefits that tourism brings to local communities scattered across the island. Tourism has propelled the transformation of communities across Jamaica's North shore. And it would be true to say that for local communities that have embraced tourism, the real impact has been one of significant enhancement. Sleepy little fishing villages like 'Ocho Rios' and 'Negril' 40 years ago, have been transformed into bustling resorts, and combined they now welcome more than half a million visitors each year. More than 17,000 people are employed directly in tourism in these two towns.

Cruise shipping has been attracted to Ocho Rios because of its excellent port infrastructure and wonderful attractions including the spectacular Dunn's river falls. This has meant significant benefit not just to Ocho Rios, but also to several other communities miles away from the coast.

Hence, for islands that engage in tourism, the industry provides a tremendous opportunity for development to be spread to communities that are outside the traditional resorts on the coastal strips. The benefit is equally present for towns that are neighbours to the big resorts. The major benefit of tourism in these once rural communities has been the diversification of economic activity and the creation of jobs in new services, the fastest growing element of the economy - for example, ground transportation, shopping, entertainment and catering being just a few.

Local people have been trained not just in the traditional resort skills, but also in information technology, accounting, engineering, general management and other disciplines. Many of these jobs have been created in areas that favour the poor, women and young people. Jobs have also been created in the traditional areas of agriculture, as farmers have risen to the challenge of producing goods for tourism consumption. In 1997, tourism purchased US$ 51 million of locally produced agricultural supplies. Manufacturing also benefited to the tune of US$ 96 million in 1997. Another US$ 312 million of indirect economic activity was generated by tourism-related industries in purchases of local goods and services.

Another major benefit has been the development of community infrastructure, primarily to serve the burgeoning tourism industry. Correspondingly this resulted in improved roads, water and other services for local people. This also works the other way around, where improved facilities for local communities have created opportunities for tourism investment.

Community-based tourism is the latest positive response to development by a government that is keen to stimulate, engage, embrace and support the Jamaican people as partners, participants and beneficiaries in progress. Over the last 30 years, succeeding administrations have recognized that for tourism to develop in a sustainable way, it must be all-embracing, and this recognition has spurred action at several levels, including a recognition of the importance of maintaining the physical environment.

At the social level, government and enlightened private sector developers have sought to engage the ordinary citizens of the country as supporters and participants in creating and offering an enhanced experience for visitors. Probably the best example of this social dimension is the "Meet-The-People" programme, which was pioneered in Jamaica nearly 40 years ago. Participating visitors leave the island with a better understanding of the country and its people. Jamaica has a **repeat rate of 40% each year**, indicating the power of the relationships that are formed through this and other programmes.

It should not be surprising that over 75 per cent of accommodation in Jamaica is owned and operated by Jamaicans. Of particular benefit to small operators are the incentives given under the resort cottages act, which provides up to seven years of relief from income tax and, in some instances, duty-free importation of capital items.

People participation is also encouraged through intensive education and awareness campaigns conducted by the Jamaica tourist board. Worthy of note is the infusion programme that focuses on making tourism an important part of the school curriculum. There is also a special programme for tourism employees including hotel workers at every level, which promotes awareness of the history and culture.

The government tourism agencies have encouraged the growth of community events that celebrate and amplify the characteristics that are peculiar to their own areas. This has given rise to a series of "homecoming" celebrations and a number of food and music festivals across the island as people draw upon their own cultural, culinary and creative resources to showcase the best of Jamaica. It has also served to encourage people to maintain their own cultural uniqueness, and to develop a domestic tourism market.

Many cultural art forms have been preserved because visitors find them so appealing. The very colourful dance and music forms ranging from the old Quadrille, Dinki Minni and Mento - all of which have given rise and sustenance to the popular reggae music for which Jamaica is known - have themselves been sustained by demand generated by tourism. In a region where all countries offer sun, sand and sea, Jamaica is differentiated because of the vibrancy of its culture, a culture to which foreigners are being exposed long before they visit the country and which serves as advertising for the island.

The experiment has been extremely successful in relation to the primary objectives of increasing community involvement in tourism and developing an economic product for these neighbourhoods.

Looking to the future, Jamaica continues to be cognizant of the critical importance of ensuring that the path taken to tourism development is sustainable. This can only be achieved if the needs of Jamaicans as well as visitors are met. It must also be done in an environment where there is continuous effort to protect and improve the available resources for the benefit of future generations. In this regard, the Jamaican government has now developed a ten-year master plan that seeks to achieve:

- Growth based on a sustainable market position;
- The enhancement of visitor experience;
- Community-based development;
- The building of an inclusive industry;
- As well as environmental sustainability.

To be successful, Jamaica like other island territories, must harness the unique resources that are at its disposal, to grow the economies and compete effectively by offering the best product available.

Source: H.E. Mr. Frank Pringle, Ambassador, WTO Conference in Jeju, Republic of Korea, 2001

2.2.6 Climate change and vulnerability of SIDS

Costal environments in general and especially in SIDS are vital for tourism-based regional and local economies; therefore, climate change affecting coastal zones puts their economies at risk. Seaside tourism seems likely to suffer damage from most of the effects of climate change, notably beach erosion, higher sea levels, greater damage from sea surges and storms, and reduced water supply. However, while some regions may see a diminution of demand from the leisure traveller, others - currently less important as tourism destinations - may see an increase.

Global warming becomes a serious concern for low-lying coral atoll islands. Prone to natural disasters such as hurricanes, earthquakes and volcanic eruptions, or to economic activities that could result in the depletion of the natural resources, the fragility of small island nations is further exacerbated by unforeseen natural and environmental disasters, which can retard economic and infrastructural development and divert scarce resources to rehabilitation and reconstruction.

Concerned by the threats of climate change for tourism, the World Tourism Organization organized an international conference in collaboration with UNEP and UNFCC[2]. The Djerba Declaration on Climate Change and Tourism was prepared through consultation with the participants in the Conference. This document considers the complex relationships between tourism and climate change, and particularly the impacts that the latter are producing upon different types of tourism destinations, including islands, while not ignoring that some transport used for tourist movements and other components of the tourism industry, contribute in return to climate change. Therefore, every strategy towards sustainable tourism should also seek to reduce transport emissions. However, it has to be acknowledged that international tourists arrivals in SIDS represent a minimal percentage of world total: the total number of international arrivals to small island countries was estimated at 27.2 million in 2000, representing 3.9% (by air and sea) of the world total of 697.8 million arrivals. Air access is a major precondition for tourism development in SIDS, while the impact on climate change by tourist arrivals in SIDS is minimal, compared with the threats on costal areas and oceans territories of SIDS created by global climate change.

2 United Nations Framework Convention on Climate Change

There are a number of different impacts of climate change on **islands, coasts and beaches,** the most severe being:

- **sea level rises** cause coast and beach erosion, inundation of flood plains, rising water tables, destruction of coastal eco-systems, salinization of aquifers and, at worst, the total submersion of islands or coastal plains.
- **warmer sea temperatures** of 1- 2ºC cause coral bleaching and dying. This leads to a breakdown in the reef protection surrounding most tropical coastlines and an amenity loss for diving and snorkelling. It is predicted that coral bleaching will increase in intensity and frequency to the extent that in the Caribbean and South East Asia it will occur by 2020 and in the Pacific by 2040.
- **increasing storm frequency,** especially in conjunction with rising sea levels, leads to damage to sea defences, protective mangrove swamps and shoreline buildings, to beach erosion and causes storm-surge damage to coral reefs .

El Niño Southern-Oscillation (ENSO)

Variations in the location of warm and cold waters within the Pacific Ocean have a cyclical effect on the global climate. In recent years, the magnitude of these variations (the oscillation between the two extremes) has been increasing. The transfer of the warm waters of the western Pacific along the equator to the eastern Pacific and to the western coasts of the Americas is now referred to as "El Niño". When the opposite happens, the phenomenon is called "La Niña". Scientists have become aware that changes associated with ENSO produce large variations in weather and climate around the world from year to year. These variations are associated with floods, heat waves, fire risks and other changes, and also influence the CO_2 balance in the atmosphere.
Extensive coral bleaching occurred as a result of El Niño in 1998 and 30 large scale incidents were reported. Coral bleaching is already evident in Central America and the Caribbean, the Pacific and Indian Ocean Islands, Asia and the Red Sea. Scientists are as yet unaware of how more frequent coral bleaching events will affect reef development and species composition.

Climate change and lost tourism revenues

When in 1998 (the warmest year ever, influenced by a strong El Niño phenomenon), coral bleaching took place on the resort of Bandos Island in the Republic of Maldives, the island drew much of its tourism revenue from diving operations. In the year in question, the island experienced a 30% drop in its normal annual income from tourists' diving operations of some US$ 1 million, indicating that earnings from tourism can be affected in the very short term by climatic factors.

Source: Climate Change and Tourism, WTO, 2003

In the **Djerba Declaration on Tourism and Climate Change**, the tourism industry, including transport companies, hoteliers, tour operators, travel agents and tourist guides, are encouraged to adjust their activities, using more energy-efficient and cleaner technologies and logistics, in order to minimize as much as possible their contribution to climate change. At the same time, governments are asked to encourage the use of renewable energy sources in tourism and transport companies and activities, by facilitating technical assistance and using fiscal and other incentives.

In this context, renewable forms of energy offer a great opportunity to the tourism sector, since by using renewable sources, which are usually locally available, abundant and clean, tourism destinations can reduce the negative impacts of using fossil fuels and maintain a healthy environment;

the latter is a key requisite at most tourism destinations. At the same time, such renewable sources can create new positive economic linkages with potential local providers of energy. In islands and other isolated destinations, locally generated and renewable sources are the safest to ensure energy security at all times, minimizing dependence on distant sources.

Renewable energy and water desalination businesses, on their part, should also make an effort to promote among tourism companies the utilization of their technologies and related equipment at convenient prices and preferential terms, at least in an initial period. There is a strong need to make accessible to the thousands of small and medium sized tourism businesses the soft energy technologies and related equipment available, in a user-friendly manner. The same is valid for the supply of water and waste water treatment plants. It may be necessary to establish cooperative agreements with local authorities and tourism and hotel trade associations to achieve a higher level of penetration of such environmentally friendly technologies in the tourism sector.

Destination: Tropical Island States

Region Climate Change Predictions	Implications/Consequences for Tourism
Relatively small temperature rises	Possible submergence
Relatively small rainfall changes	Salinization of aquifers
Sea level rises critical	Reef damage and erosion
Storm frequency and intensity increases	Increasingly untenable beach resorts
Coral bleaching	Ingress of new tropical diseases Increased energy costs for A/C
Islands	Reduced demand for holidays to worst affected Reduced demand for dive holidays

Source: Travel Research International, WTO Conference on Climate Change, Djerba/2003

The increase in awareness on sustainability questions and the high technological progress achieved in many areas including energy and water related issues, compared to the tangible progress in implementing sustainable practices is still limited. Some examples of good practices do exist, but still remain exceptions if compared to the tourism industry as a whole. In this regard, one of the main challenges is how to move from these paradigmatic case studies that have usually been promoted and developed by private pioneers or with external UN or NGO support, to a widespread adoption of such exemplary practices. How to transfer to the policy level such good examples, mainstreaming good practice into the entire tourism industry.

While the impacts of climate change vary and are likely to manifest themselves in a variety of ways, what is certain is that the tourism sector has to show itself adaptable to changing conditions. Some changes may indeed favour an increase in tourism – such as warmer, drier summers in Northern Europe leading to greater domestic travel and a reverse flow of tourists from the South – so that one destination's loss is another's gain. However, the majority of changes, rising temperatures and sea levels and increasing storm frequency, present the industry, and more specifically small island nations, with real challenges.

2.3 Challenges for an adapted tourism policy

Tourism growth, while much desired, also brings with it increased pressure on the environment and local communities. Considering the scarcity of resources, small island developing states are in a very critical situation, which requires the creation of a certain number of rules and principles.

In the Caribbean, many islands like the Bahamas, Cuba, the Dominican Republic and Jamaica are rethinking their future strategies in tourism. In these islands, tourism has entered its mature stage and has become one of the economic pillars, contributing in many cases for more than one third of gross national product (GNP).

In Asia and the Pacific, tourism is attaining significant levels in the small island States of Fiji, Vanuatu, Papua New Guinea, Samoa, the Cook Islands and Maldives, but is encountering developmental difficulties in some, such as Kiribati, Tonga and Tuvalu.

In the African region, while Seychelles and Mauritius have revised their policies to raise the quality of their tourism product, other islands, such as Sao Tome and Principe, Cape Verde and the Comoros, are seeking to strengthen their own tourism development programmes.

The following example should provide a new avenue in considering mass tourism and the balance between negative and positive impacts for an island nation.

Can mass tourism be a driving force behind poverty alleviation and the promotion of the local economy?

The German Technical Cooperation (GTZ) coordination office for Latin America and the Caribbean started different initiatives focussing on the potential of mass tourism for sustainable development. One of these was the so-called "Sustainable All-inclusive?" initiative, starting with a research on the economic interaction of All-inclusive resorts with the local economy and communities. Altogether this interaction was studied in 7 resorts with a total of 2,500 rooms in the Dominican Republic, Jamaica and Nicaragua. The conclusions of this study are summarized below:

In the last two decades tourism - and especially mass tourism - has always been something like a 'poor cousin' for development politicians: rather not deal with and talk about it, otherwise the critics from the fundamentalist anti-travel-corner will pull us into pieces again anyway. Tourism destroys the environment and culture; sex-tourism and bawling half-naked tourists on the beaches of the Caribbean paradise - is this supposed to be useful for the country and alleviate poverty?
It is high time to convert this ignorance of the development community vis-à-vis mass tourism into a productive win-win partnership. One of the most important and underestimated issues is the function of mass and luxury tourism as a generator of jobs and a way of combating poverty.

To resume our results, we would like to present the following statements:

1. Tourism creates jobs – not only for chambermaids and waiters

All jobs at the facilities surveyed are occupied by locals - except for a few in the senior management and those in the entertainment section that demand special skills (e.g. diving instructors). Besides, there is a very diversified hierarchy with good prospects of promotion and salary perspectives for those who usually start as semi-skilled simple workers in the service area. Often, the starting salaries are nominally on the level of the minimum wage (e.g. almost US$ 100 in the Dominican Republic). Nevertheless, taking into account the share in the obligatory tip (10%), which is generally put on the hotel price, this income rises on average by 50-70%. If counting in the other benefits and services (social and health insurance, free transport and meals) as well, it amounts to a minimum gross salary of more than US$ 200, that is more than twice as much as the minimum wage. Especially in comparison to other opportunities for earning money in the country, this is a very attractive starting salary (e.g. agricultural workers, such as in the sugar-cane industry, earn only one US$ per day; all-inclusive employees in a Central American country earn more than teachers and twice as much as the employees of the small restaurants and hotels next door).

2. Tourism gives development decisive impetus and promotes the diversification of the local industry and commerce

Why two big Jamaican hotel chains or a tourist resort with 18,000 hotel rooms in the Dominican Republic might be a better and more sustainable contribution to the alleviation of poverty than many donor programs.

Why 10 big sustainably planned and managed beach hotels might benefit poor people and the environment in Nicaragua than the costly monitoring of the PRSP - process by the sponsorship community.

If every tourist staying in a big hotel facility in Mexico spends only one US$ more per day outside in the local economy, US$ 60 million would flow into the local economy resulting in the reduction of poverty (which is much more than Germany gives as development aid to that country).

3. Tourism consumes only a minor part of the environment and natural resources and is able to help saving the major part of it

Whenever big holiday resorts are built, it is in fact a massive intervention in nature and the environment at the building site. Accordingly, no tourism is always better than any kind of tourism. This, however, applies to every form of economic activity: no agriculture is always better than the most highly polished eco-farming, because even eco-farming always involves intervention in nature and the environment.

This is why the question of (mass) tourism or not is wrongly posed. It schould be:

If a country cannot afford the luxury of not having any significant economic activity that earns foreign currency, it has to decide whether export agriculture, mining, oil / energy industry, refining wages / assembling for large combines or precisely tourism, consumes a minor or major part of the environment compared

- with how many jobs and income is being created;
- to what extent it contributes to alleviate poverty;
- how many women find an employment which positive contributions they make to the building up of a national economy.

Unfortunately, development politics has not been deeply and, above all, not systematically and strategically concerned with these issues up to now, although this is, considering the paramount significance of worldwide tourism as the sector with the highest turnover, one of the central issues for sustainable alleviation of poverty and local economic development.

Source: Klaus Lengefeld, Coordination Unit Latin America & the Caribbean, GTZ, 2004

Given the dynamism of the industry and acknowledging their high vulnerability and dependence on tourism, SIDS have embarked on adapted initiatives aimed at building a wider, more sustainable base of support for the tourism industry among the local population, promoting participatory action and a sense of ownership in order to ensure the success of the industry.

The challenges of a new island tourism policy are viewed from other perspectives:

- **establish limits and conditions of tourism development** to be compatible economically, territorially, socially, culturally, and environmentally;
- **achieve the best possible integration of tourism** within the island system as a whole, above all in the economic area, including advancement of certain traditional sectors and diversification of the economic system;
- **define a strategy and tourism products** that will maximize opportunities like ecotourism, nature based tourism, rural tourism, etc.;
- **reduce impacts**, and not overwhelm the carrying capacities of fragile island systems;
- **modulate, finance, and ensure the quality of infrastructure** and tourism projects;
- **improve the profitability of tourism investment**, lengthen the tourist season, increase the length of stay and the number of overnight stays;
- **achieve customer loyalty**, improve occupancy rates, increase tourist spending;
- **bring a fair distribution of the profits and costs of tourism among the main stakeholders**: direct participants (tour operators, hotel keepers, etc.), those who care for natural and cultural attractions (farmers, local community), and the public institutions responsible for the establishment and **upkeep of public services** and environmental quality on the island.

An appropriate and adapted policy formulation and planning would imply selecting a desirable future out of a range of plausible alternatives, and implementing strategies and actions that will achieve the desired outcome in developing tourism sustainably. Thus, by definition, planning moves us from the present to the future. It is critical, therefore, that planners and tourism operators understand social, political and economic trends, as these form the context for planning. Such understanding provides opportunities to capitalize on emerging markets, develop actions that are more efficient and effective, and ensure that strategies and actions can be adapted to changing conditions.

Chapter 3

Islands and the challenge of accessibility

Islands differ greatly in size, climate, natural resources, access, habitation, culture, history, land tenure, legal systems and economic activity, including tourism. However, they also have certain characteristics in common: their physical isolation from mainland neighbours and the problem of access by air or by sea; hence, the heavy dependence on imports as a result of limited natural resource endowment; and fragile environments.

The biggest problem faced by small island communities is that of access. Given the limited scale of an island community and its economic outputs, there is often an absence of economies of scale that would provide a rationale for frequent and reliable transportation services. This holds true for both micro-states and off-shore islands.

The isolated and remote nature of many SIDS means that transport and communications are central to maintain contact and linkages with the rest of the world. For SIDS, adequate transportation access from main generating markets to the tourism area and a functional transportation network to serve attractions and tourist facilities within islands are essential for developing tourism.

It is therefore necessary to combine the application of environmentally-responsible island policies with the procurement of international recognition of their exceptional dependence on transport to and from the island.

3.1 Air Transport

The formulation and implementation of an air transport policy that is responsive to the needs of the tourism industry is of critical importance for small island states.

It is essential to take into account how important it is to provide, maintain and complement air links with the major tourist generating markets in order to ensure continuous accessibility and to sustain the island tourism industry, as well as to provide a domestic air service in support of the development of the other islands of the archipelago, and ground-handling services.

Consideration should be given to national economic interests, especially the needs and demands of the tourism industry, and the need to maintain adequate freight capacity. To this end, a close consultation with all stakeholders is necessary to continuously review air transport policy in order to ensure that air access matches the targets for increased visitor arrivals.

Some islands have no adequate air access, therefore they cannot develop tourism. Some are facing another phase of development were low cost airlines serve a mass tourism industry that has reached a maturity stage with the problems of carrying capacity, numbers and yield.

The development of air transport in small islands may have a considerable impact on their environment too. The creation and development of air links involves the construction of airports, often in sites which are considered most suitable to meet the requirements of air transport especially with respect to safety. For this reason runways are often built close to the coast and this may affect the equilibrium of coastal ecosystems as in mangrove swamps or near natural beaches.

Tourism development in islands requires the harmonization between policies for developing air transport and those for tourism. For tourism development to be sustainable, the tourism demand for air transport must tie in with the supply of airline companies. However, such adaptation is difficult to achieve because the interests of air transport and those of tourism tend to differ. Tourism professionals usually call for increasingly low prices for increasingly large numbers of tourists. But air carriers need to take into account production costs, which are generally higher in islands, as well as the requirements with respect to flight regularity and frequency of the local island populations.

Thus, it is especially difficult to determine a strategy for air transport for islands and there is a risk that the objectives of sustainable tourism development will not be met. A supply of mass air transport may bring with it the development of mass tourism which in turn may disrupt the fragile environmental and social equilibrium existing on islands. The choice between regular and charter air transport, as well as deregulation of air transport, are the major challenges for the future of tourism in islands and its continuance.

3.1.1 Charter and low-cost air transport and tourism

Because of the overall importance of tourism in SIDS, access by air is therefore an essential condition for the development of tourism. The inconvenient and limited, as well as the high cost of air access from some existing and potential tourist markets, and inadequate airport infrastructure, particularly for international arrivals, are issues that must be given a high priority.

International tourism has undergone many changes in the age of the jet. New aviation technology has made it possible to develop distant markets for tourism, and tourism between continents is flourishing. The steady fall of prices in real terms over the years has helped to popularize air travel. **Charter flights** have contributed much to this development; not only they have helped to open new markets, but they have also done much to satisfy the seasonal nature of tourism demand, in particular by making peak capacity available during the high season. Charter flights have also bypassed the obstacles of bilateral regulation and the price cartel of the industry.

The introduction of **charter flights** is a striking manifestation of access by the middle classes in developed countries to leisure and international travel, in various forms. By dint of their numerous customers, tour operators have gained considerable commercial strength allowing them to negotiate, from a favorable position, the purchase of seats from the airlines. In other cases, powerful groups have emerged through vertical integration, a tour operator creating or incorporating a specialist airline and, at the same time, endeavoring to control its distribution network.

The strong **price elasticity** of demand for holiday travel explains this formula's success, its constraints notwithstanding. This economic fact, which is borne out by history, remains just as true today: broadly speaking, **the tourism industry profits from the lower cost of air transport and, at the same time, air transport wins new customers.** Low-cost airlines have demonstrated unequivocally that low fares stimulate travel.

3.1.2 Defining an adequate air transport policy for SIDS

The technical and commercial changes occurring in the airline industry, whether these concern types of aircraft or computerized reservations, have influenced price levels, the relative cost of destinations, readiness of access to them and thus distribution channels. Consequently, they bring about profound changes in the tourism industry.

- the increases in both international tourist arrivals and air travel are too parallel to be merely coincidental; they are proof of the strong interdependence between the two sectors;

- tourism was not the priority of the traditional system of organizing air transport; it has often developed on the sidelines of this system, and in parallel with the democratization of access to leisure activities;
- the legal, technical and economic changes in the traditional system are today a source of benefits but also of uncertainty for consumers and the tourism industry;
- multilateralism continues to be a constant concern, but is a reality constantly postponed;
- the changes that took place in the past will tend to continue, if not in exactly the same way;
- tourism policies can and must reflect more faithfully the dimension of the airline industry and its development; transport policies, for their part, should increasingly take account of the tourism factor.

Looking at the long term, the similarity of trends is striking: globally as well as regionally, international tourist arrivals and the number of passengers on international scheduled airlines have progressed at the same pace, even if it these last years of crisis since 2001 show that air transport may, at times, be more vulnerable than tourism as a whole.

It is clear that air transport has contributed to the development of capacity and the emergence of new resorts. Frequently the prospect of easy access by air may be regarded as the trigger of tourism development. Most tourist destinations in the Caribbean, the Indian Ocean and Asia-Pacific would not have taken off without that prospect. Both are highly dependent on the business cycle. When income is stagnating or indeed falling then demand also falls or at least ceases to rise. In both air transport and tourism, revenues and prices tend to be elastic.

The tourism industry has much to gain from the existence of an air transport market, which would be open, competitive and transparent. Some of the trends already identified are clearly set to persist and to continue influencing the relations between air transport and the tourism industry. But they will undoubtedly do so in different ways.

- **The parallel growth of the two sectors is likely to continue.**
- **Privatization, globalization and liberalization will tend by their very nature to apply worldwide.** It is clear that even if the negotiation of traffic rights was excluded from the GATS agreement, developing countries as SIDS will be under increasing pressure to ensure that their national airlines follow this general trend.

The governments of countries seeking to develop their tourism industries will thus be faced with an alternative. For them the simplest solution is to allow, or even to encourage, the privatization of their national carriers and permit them to form groupings and become integrated into future transnational mega-carriers. This is necessary if they are to take advantage of the liberalization process and benefit from the increased productivity generated by such alliances.

But this is often also the path of satellization and loss of identity. The question therefore arises whether the macro-economic benefits to be gained, particularly by the tourism industry, justify what may be seen as an abandonment of control of the national carrier.

The issue of the tourism-air transport link will therefore seem very different according to whether one is analysing long-haul, North-South movements from the developed generating countries to distant holiday areas in developing countries, or otherwise.

The most characteristic case is that of islands with considerable tourism potential and remote from the generating markets, which often stake their all on tourism. Examples of such situations may be found in Asia, the Indian Ocean and the Pacific.

For destinations where the process of tourism increase is lengthy, the policy-makers and the operational sector of tourism spontaneously call the airlines to account, accusing them of applying insufficiently attractive fares or of failing to provide the necessary capacity - in short of being unable to anticipate demand. In reply, the airlines explain that concern for normal profitability means they have to worry about filling their aircraft and that they would be prepared to provide additional seats, more attractive fares and even charter flights if there were a proven solvent demand for them.

The debate is not merely academic. It is of interest to a number of destinations remote from the generating markets, which have difficulty in reaching the stage where a cumulative process is established and where tourism and air transport support each other mutually in their growth.

In the configuration of an island economy, albeit strongly tourism-oriented but remote from the generating markets, the public authorities generally face two questions: with limited resources, should they invest as a priority in the inbound tourism industry or in air transport? Should the national carrier be protected from outside competition that is too keen for it at the risk of limiting tourist arrivals?

In this specific area, WTO's work has brought clear replies:

- **The tourism industry generates more income: in the proportion of 2.5 to 1;**
- **provides many more jobs: in the proportion of 12 to 1; and**
- **produces fewer leakages in the form of related imports: in the ratio of 1 to 4, than the national air carrier.**

Thus, the public authorities would be mistaken if they were systematically to give priority to the short-term interests of the national carrier.

It is however true to say that, in most countries, aviation lobbies are more capable of making themselves heard by the authorities than is the tourism industry, which is less organized.

All this underscores the **synergies** between aviation and tourism. But there is also a risk of **conflict** between the policies pertaining to these two sectors even if they are related. As the study prepared for WTO emphasizes: "The most fundamental conflicts are those which arise from policies designed to protect national airlines from foreign competition. Such protection can lead to the support of inefficient operations, to restrictions on the services provided and to higher fares. Policies of this kind can lead to a reduction in the number of tourist visitors to the country and to a loss of the economic benefits from this business. These losses may be greater than the advantages gained by the national economies from the protection of the national airline."

However, as the same study points out, "it is not always true that the tourism losses will be greater than the gains from protectionist aviation policies. There are good reasons why it may be beneficial for a country, particularly a developing country, to protect its own national airline. And it is not always true that an increase in tourist visitors is beneficial: there are environmental and other factors which may be negative factors in this equation."

That is why it is essential to develop an analytical framework within which any country can measure the benefits and losses of alternative aviation and tourism policies and thus make logical decisions about which is best.

Mauritius: a successful aviation policy

Air transport to the island of Mauritius can be considered one of the best examples of adaptation in line with the development of up-market tourism. Air Mauritius has been equipped with the most modern, high-performance craft allowing it to set up non-stop air links with the main tourism markets for the island, namely France, Switzerland, Germany, Belgium and the United Kingdom, as well as with South Africa, Australia, India and South-East Asia.

This strategy for developing air transport has made it possible to diversify the types of tourists received and to extend the tourist season throughout the year. It was implemented within the framework of regular air transport which has made it possible to increase flight frequency and capacity to meet the needs of the tourism market.

Thus, the development of tourism on the island of Mauritius can be considered relatively invulnerable, to the extent that the Air Mauritius airline has developed in line with the tourism sector of the island.

Source: WTO Lanzarote Conference on SIDS, 1998

3.1.3 Regional policies

For SIDS, tourism can be a very useful way of pursuing an effective regional air transport policy because, unlike other industries, the consumer of tourism has to come to the production area and, hence, creates the activity there.

Transportation linkages between countries in each region are complicated by a lack of coordination of airline schedules, often requiring indirect travel through de facto hubs. Regional policies can often help to effectively address this problem, hampering trade and tourism development. Some regions in the world have overcome this problem by creating efficient regional routes and regional airlines.

The example of Barbados is relevant. Barbados has developed a different strategy for air transport based on two multinational airline companies, by joining up with Trinidad and Tobago and Saint Lucia, namely BWIA for long and medium distances and LIAT for short distances between the islands.

This strategy has allowed the development of direct links (non-stop) between Bridgetown and Europe, North America and South America as well as with islands in the south of the Caribbean, mainly Grenada, Saint Vincent and the Grenadines, Trinidad and Tobago, Saint Lucia, Dominica and Antigua and Barbuda.

This double air transport network could be considered especially suitable for the diversified, international, up-market tourism of Barbados which received 498,000 international tourists in 2002.

Associations between airlines present a real commercial advantage in that they respect the independence of each of the partners for management while bringing with them substantial reductions in commercial costs and greater capacity on certain lines based on code sharing agreements. Such agreements allow companies to reorganize their networks and their sales systems within the framework of a worldwide partnership.

With such worldwide strategies for associations between airlines, companies in small island states may have a new role to play by participating in such associations, offering complementary regional services, like BWIA and LIAT in the Caribbean, which offer many connections for flights by the main North American companies, especially American Airlines.

The Caribbean islands

The example of the Caribbean shows that the development of international tourism in islands can take place by adapting regular air transport, with charter traffic playing only an additional role.

This situation is the result of policies drawn up jointly by the authorities in charge of tourism development and by the airline companies. Three types of strategy are currently being applied in the Caribbean islands and can be described through the example of Puerto Rico.

The case of **Puerto Rico** can be considered an example of one of the main successes of the strategy to create a tourism and air travel hub in island regions. The airport of San Juan is the entry point for most of the main North American airline companies in the Caribbean but at the same time, because of the policy adopted by American Airlines, acts as a hub from which flights leave for the small islands to the north and south of Puerto Rico.

American Airlines invested over one billion dollars in setting up its own airport facilities in Puerto Rico and in establishing a base for its subsidiary, American Eagle, in order to offer several daily flights to most of the destinations in the Caribbean from Puerto Rico.

This strategy allows American Airlines to lead the market between the United States and the Caribbean islands while Puerto Rico benefits from being the nerve centre and gateway for the Caribbean as a whole.

In 2002 Puerto Rico was the main tourism destination in the Caribbean with 3.3 million tourist arrivals (i.e. excluding one-day visitors), followed by the Dominican Republic with 2.8 million. Puerto Rico has also become, thanks to these air facilities, the main point of departure after Miami for cruises to the other islands of the Caribbean.

However, the growth in tourism arrivals is still low with respect to other island destinations in the Caribbean and in other parts of the world.

Source: F. Vellas, WTO Lanzarote Conference on SIDS, 1998, data updated for 2002

Another example is that of Air Pacific, which has generated an increase of international tourist arrivals for the entire South Pacific region and its micro island states.

Air Pacific and Fiji's tourism industry are inextricably linked

Air Pacific has a controlling related party relationship with its major shareholder, the Government of the Republic of the Fiji Islands, and has a commercial agreement with Qantas Airways Limited, also a stakeholder, that includes code share agreements on various routes, leasing of aircraft and obtaining engineering services.

The shares of Air Pacific are distributed as follows:

Government of Fiji	51.00%

Qantas Airways Limited	46.32%
Air New Zealand Limited	1.94%
Government of Kiribati	0.27%
Government of Tonga	0.27%
Government of Samoa	0.12%
Government of Nauru	0.08%

Flexibility, speed of response, cost minimization and quality management information are key strategies for Air Pacific.

The Chairman of Air Pacific, Mr Gerald Barrack, CF, CBE, announced that Air Pacific achieved a milestone profit of $34.6 million before tax and $24.5 million after tax for the financial year ending 31 March 2004. This is a growth of 37.8% pre-tax and 48.6% post-tax compared to the 2002/03 profit.

Revenue increased by $14.2 million to $421.7 million, an increase of 3.5% whilst costs increased by $9.36 million [2.5%] to $384.188 million. The Board has declared a dividend of 19 cents [$4.958 million] and approved payment of a bonus to all staff. In addition to being the highest profit ever recorded by Air Pacific, the airline, for the first time, carried more than half a million customers in one year [541,000].

The result was pleasing given the severe traffic impact from the SARS crisis and the Iraq war. These events impacted tourism and travel, particularly from Japan and North America and those markets are yet to fully recover.

Two Boeing 747-400 aircraft were introduced into the fleet in April and June 2003 which permitted growth by Air Pacific to daily B747 services to Sydney, the addition of a fourth weekly service to Los Angeles and expansion of flying into Melbourne, Brisbane and Auckland, including the introduction of B747 and B767 services to Auckland and Brisbane.

During the year, the Boeing 737-700 leased to Qantas the preceding year was returned to Air Pacific which enabled the Company to increase and improve services to Apia (Samoa), Nukualofa (Tonga) and Port Vila (Vanuatu).

Commitment to the Environment

As a concerned corporate citizen, Air Pacific is committed to environmental awareness and to ensuring that the Company acts in a responsible manner where environmental issues are involved. Whilst the concept and process of environmental reporting is a relatively new discipline in this part of the world, Air Pacific is keen to take a proactive stance in handling environmental risk management issues on a progressive basis. We ensure that our fleet of aircraft meets the specific environmental certification standards on emissions, developed by ICAO.

Air Pacific's overall commitment is to the maintenance and promotion of a clean and pure environment. We will continue to practice recycling wherever possible, for its economic and environmental benefits, and to reduce waste material and engine emission.
By taking such a proactive stance we hope that we can serve as a positive role model for all other companies we deal with as well as focussing attention on this important issue.

Source: Chairman of Air Pacific, Mr Gerald Barrack, 2003

3.1.4 Major challenges facing international air transport

These last years of crisis have underlined how critical is the need to comprehensively address the issues of safety and security for tourists, since any shortcomings in this area have the potential to jeopardize all the gains made in other areas.

A pragmatic and flexible approach towards air liberalization, taking account of the wider national interest of air safety and efficiency, in accordance with the recommendations and practices of the International Civil Aviation Organization (ICAO), must be adopted in order to promote island tourism destinations in generating markets. For this purpose, in line with the ICAO recommendations, **regional centres for training in air safety in island regions might be considered essential for the sustainable development of international tourism in islands.**

As tourism will not flourish to destinations in civil turmoil, at war, or where tourists' health or security is perceived to be under threat, safety of travel should be included as a fundamental or foundation factor. Conflict, disaster and incidents can strongly influence tourism's health and growth. A lot depends on how such negative events are dealt with. Experience in different parts of the world has shown repeatedly **that tourism almost without exception turns out to be very resilient and manifests a strong capacity for recovery.**

- **Safety:** There has been a long-term decline in the number of fatal accidents in international aviation as technologies have evolved and ICAO Safety Standards have been developed. Aviation is also safer, on most criteria, than other forms of transport. Over the past ten years, accident rates have shown a levelling off. Efforts to reduce these rates are imperative to avoid an increase in accidents as traffic continues to grow. The major issue in the future will be **the coordination and transfer of regulatory responsibility** arising from globalization, the emergence of regional and sub-regional blocs, the commercialization of service providers.

- **Security:** Aviation is subject to several forms of security concerns ranging from conventional forms of terrorism, such as hijacking and ground attacks at airports and new forms such as found in the behaviour of unruly passengers. Aviation security has become a high priority area for governments, air carriers, manufacturers and service providers alike. The security issues will largely parallel those facing safety with increased emphasis necessary on maintaining **an adequate global security network.**

- **Environment:** Air transport will continue facing increasingly intense pressures to reduce noise around the airports and the emissions of aircraft. With no foreseeable replacement for fossil fuels as the predominant energy source for aircraft operations, air transport's contribution to global warming, which is small but significant, may continue to grow, leading to demands for operational restrictions and taxation and other levies, including market based constraints. ICAO is presently seen as the focal point for the harmonization of aviation environmental regulation worldwide, notably as regards emissions through the 1997 Kyoto Protocol to the United Nations Framework Convention on Climate Change.

- **Infrastructure:** Aviation is dependent on an extensive and highly sophisticated infrastructure embracing airport facilities, air traffic control and air navigation systems. Proliferation of air traffic will result in an insufficient coverage of airports and surrounding airspace. From an economic perspective the constraints placed on airports will have a direct bearing on traffic growth and will act as an inhibitor to the achievement of total market access. The developing countries, especially those with low volume of traffic will face some difficulties in financing their infrastructure. The world requirements of Airports and Air Navigation services providers are estimated to exceed US$ 300 billion, from now to the year 2010.

- **Information technology:** has emerged as a key influence in air transport in the fields of distribution, security and facilitation. Machine readable travel documents including the "smart card" and the use of biometric applications are tools that improve passenger and cargo flows at airports, while at the same time ensuring security against fraudulent document usage. With the

Computer Reservation Systems and the development of Internet ticket sales, the Global distribution systems is facing unprecedented challenge. The facilitation of booking travel and tourism through **electronic technology** is leading more suppliers to seek to increase their direct sales. While household access to the Internet in most countries is not yet widespread, penetration levels of 50 per cent are widely predicted by 2010.

3.1.5 Future global trends in air transport

WTO's *Vision 2020* shows that key development factors will be of importance for SIDS in the future, while harmonizing their strategies in the context of tourism development and their dependence on air transport. The process of concentration of power within the sub-sectors which make up the travel and tourism sector is continuing apace. While regulatory intervention or corporate incompatibility may thwart their ambitions, if the major airlines achieve their objectives, most passenger flights will take place on one of just three airline groups before 2010. The danger for travellers will be if the three groups unofficially divide up the world between them, creating such strong spheres of influence that competitors dare not challenge them and, in consequence, fares rise.

These new strategies are not entirely dictated by financial considerations, they are one of the main consequences of the liberalization of air transport and the resulting globalization. In the context of deregulation which authorizes free access to the market on all air routes, established airlines must try to position themselves on their traditional market.

On the other hand, the new strategies pursued are aimed at ensuring the loyalty of the customer by offering more services than competitors. For this reason, airlines are today re-focusing their activities and above all their investments on air transport in particular the alliance-building strategy, the creation of hubs, the constitution of global distribution services, frequent flier programmes and the renewal of fleets and privatization.

- In addition to **horizontal and vertical integration**, many travel and tourism companies are utilizing a diagonal integration strategy, whereby they establish operations to offer products and services which tourists commonly purchase but which are not directly part of the tourism product, e.g. insurance, currency, luggage and other travel goods.
- Airlines, hotel groups, tour operators, car rental firms - all are examining the **reduction of the levels of standard commission paid to travel agents**, arguing that the speed and ease of bookings through their computer reservation systems do not warrant retention of the original rates which reflected more time input on the agents' part.
- **Frequent flier programmes** are today one of the principal marketing and promotion tools created by airlines. They enable better information about clients to be obtained and ensure that promotional activities are better focused. Launched by American Airlines, frequent flier programmes today have over 100 million members and are the subject of keen competition between airlines.
- The destinations that deal most effectively with negative events will best limit their impact. In general, harm can be considerably reduced with **appropriate communication strategies** and by an open and sensible approach addressing the problems clearly and professionally instead of trying to deny them.
- On the other hand, however, it will be a challenge in itself to deal with the shadow sides of the anticipated increased demand. Much depends on the capability to address **problems related to congestion, delays, pollution and safety.**
- **Technological advances** are expected to continue to affect the field of transport technology. Commercial jet aircraft technology made flying to foreign destinations technically possible and affordable for an increasingly large proportion of the population. More fuel efficient aircraft progressively reduced real costs of international travel. Future developments are for ever larger

capacity aircraft and better availability of appropriate aircraft, that is, seats and other facilities and performance related to a wide variety of route types, which permit better "matching" of aircraft types according to demand. The implication is yet cheaper air travel, not at the rate achieved in the 70s and 80s, but nonetheless some additional cost reduction.

By expanding their geographic operations as well as the range of products and services offered, the major travel and tourism global groupings will increasingly be able to meet the needs of a greater proportion of the travelling public (and the many market segments and origin- destination routes which make up the total travel and tourism markets). **By utilizing their economies of both scale and scope, they will be able to provide these at value-for-money price levels which smaller (or less extensive like in SIDS) competitors cannot match.** With a powerful hold on their markets achieved, it remains to be seen if these groups will then exploit this control by moving prices up or whether consumer and destination interest groups will exert sufficient influence on the mega-suppliers to maintain rates at levels which stimulate continued strong demand growth.

3.2 Cruise Tourism

Unlike the traditional transatlantic travel on ocean liners, modern cruise tourism is above all characterized by the transformation of the vessel from mere means of transport to a destination in itself. The cruise ship serves as a floating hotel offering an attractive, convenient and hassle-free way to see multiple destinations without having to change accommodation, and neither to fly or travel by land. The starting point for this category of leisure tourism can be found in the early 1970s when the first modern cruises began to operate in the Caribbean with North American clientele.

In the 1990s, the cruise phenomenon reached the United Kingdom followed by many other countries in Europe and in Asia and the Pacific. On board, passengers are generally provided with full-board style accommodation and can enjoy a broad range of facilities such as restaurants, bars, meeting rooms, disco, casino, swimming pools, sauna, jacuzzi, gym and other sports facilities, body and beauty services, cinema, theatre, library, children's activities and duty free shops.

As a result of the trend towards the operation of ever-larger vessels with even more facilities, cruise ships have in fact developed from floating hotels to floating resorts. For this reason the main competitors are considered the land resorts and not so much the other cruise lines.

3.2.1 Islands are of particular interest for cruise tourism

Cruising tourism refers to time spent on a waterborne vessel for leisure purposes. This tends to imply trips during which the passenger is primarily based on a vessel that travels to a number of destinations, mostly islands, where they disembark for short periods to visit land based sites.

In 2000, worldwide cruise demand reached 9.6 million passengers. With an average number of nights of 6.9 per cruise trip, the total number of nights amounted to 67 million. In both cases the share of **the cruise sector is calculated at about 1.5 per cent of worldwide tourism demand.**

Although the cruise sector in relative terms still only represents a modest share of worldwide tourism, it is noteworthy that when considered as a destination on its own, cruise tourism already meets up with established destination countries. At the same time cruise operators had some 200 thousands berths on offer, **the cruise industry representing just 0.6% of the world's accommodation capacity,** it would seem that the importance of the cruise business is minimal.

However, there are other figures that must be taken into account in order to form a clearer picture of its importance:

- **the high level of business confidence in the industry is reflected in operators' order books (worth over 13 billion dollars);**
- **high present and future growth rates (8% per year);**
- **tourist consumption generated at destinations;**
- **the possibility of opening up new destinations for land-based tourism due to the intense desire created by cruises to return to the destination; and**
- **high added value of cruises.**

These aspects give an idea of the effects of this new form of holiday. Therefore, its importance lies not so much in the size of the cruise business per se, but rather in the activity's effects.

Basic data cruise sector in comparison to international tourism worldwide, 2000

	Cruise sector	Int. tourism	Cruise sect./Int. tourism
Volume			
Total passengers / tourists (million)	9.6	697	1.4%
Berths/Beds on offer (million)	0.2	34	0.6%
Demand (million nights)	67	3,500	1.9%
Average number of nights	6.9	5	
Revenue/Int Tourism Receipts			
Total revenue (US$ billion)	13	477	2.7%
Average per passenger / tourist (US$)	1,341	685 [a]	
Average per night (US$)	193	136 [a]	

[a] In case of international tourism receipts averages are overestimated as it also include receipts from same-day visits

Source: compilation from WTO and data G.P.Wild (International) Limited used in WTO (2003)

The cruise ship industry is a rapidly growing tourism segment, with more and larger ships visiting increasing numbers of destinations, ranging from large cities to the most remote regions and cultures on the planet. Although North America is a relatively more developed and mature market, accounting for almost 2/3 of demand, it still has substantial potential demand, which the Cruiseline International Association has estimated at some 43.5 million tourists over the next five years, showing good potential for growth and expansion. (Worldwide Cruise ship Activity, WTO, 2003).

Demand from the US (with three major sources: New York, South Atlantic and Pacific) and Canada more than doubled between 1980 and 1990 and almost doubled again in the decade to reach 6.9 million passengers in 2000.

However, in the period 1990-2000 demand outside the region grew almost twice as fast, but of course from much lower base volumes. Demand from Europe increased from 600 thousand passengers in 1990 to 1.9 million in 2000, raising the share of the market from 14 to 20 per cent. The main European market is the United Kingdom with 740 thousand passengers in 2000, followed by Germany, Italy, France and Spain; the remaining 8 per cent of demand, corresponding to 800 thousand passengers, originate mostly from Asia with as principal sources Japan, the Republic of Korea and Taiwan.

Cruise itineraries offered reflect to a fair extent the current structure of demand, as operators prefer to choose base ports relatively close to major source markets. As a reaction to the reluctance to flying post 11 September, this trend is even reinforced to the benefit of ports such as New York. The Caribbean, mostly served from base ports in Florida, are still by some distance the busiest cruise region, in particular during the winter months of the predominantly northern hemisphere source markets.

One of the advantages of cruise operators over their land-based competition is their flexibility to adapt itineraries to demand. Seasonality is thus hardly a problem for the cruise industry. By season a substantial relocation of fleets from one region to another can be observed. In summertime cruise lines include Northern destinations such as Alaska and Atlantic Europe, while in wintertime they can be found in (sub)tropical zones or in the Southern hemisphere.

In summer, the Caribbean is only second destination region after the Mediterranean. The European share decreases substantially in wintertime to the benefit of not only the Caribbean but also Western Mexico and Asia and the Pacific. Furthermore, also Southern America and the Indian Ocean are added to the supply on offer as specific winter destinations.

Many of the destinations, in particular in the Caribbean, record substantial numbers of cruise passengers:

- **Five island destinations reported over one million arrivals each in 2002: the ratio of cruise passengers to tourists staying overnight ranges up to 5 times as many.**
  - Bahamas: 2.8 million;
  - US Virgin Islands: 1.7 million;
  - Cayman Islands: 1.6 million;
  - Puerto Rico: 1.3 million (with the port of San Juan not only serving as destination port but also as a major base port for itineraries in the southern part of the Caribbean) ;
  - St Maarten: 1 million.

- **Cruise passengers exceed the number of land-based tourists by two times in:**
  - Cayman Islands;
  - Dominica;
  - Haiti;
  - Saint Kitts and Nevis;
  - Saint Maarten;
  - Saint Vincent and the Grenadines; and
  - US Virgin Islands.

Between 1990 and 2002, various destinations such as Dominica, Belize and Panama, entered the cruise market developing from virtually no cruise passengers to a hundred thousand or several hundred thousand. Many other destinations recorded double-digit growth rates in the same period, tripling or quadrupling passenger numbers from an already larger base.

- **The strongest growers, currently receiving over 200,000 passengers a year:**
  - Saint Lucia (12% a year to 387 thousand);
  - Dominican Republic (14% a year to 247 thousand);
  - Aruba (13% a year to 582 thousand);
  - Costa Rica (12% a year to 222 thousand); and
  - Cayman Islands (13% a year).

In times of uncertainty for the tourism industry, cruise ships are still performing well and during the last decade, the cruise industry has been the tourism sub-sector with the highest growth rate.

Many island destinations that are developing their tourism product or are in the process of establishing themselves as world tourism destinations often try to attract cruise vessels to call at their ports.

Although revenue is not generated through accommodation, arriving visitors do tend to spend money in the local markets and souvenir shops. Cuba is currently attracting cruise ships to its waters, and some emerging destinations are looking at the possibility. However, a cautious approach has to be adopted while estimating the impacts and benefits of cruise tourism for an island destination. More accurate research and data in this domain would help island destination to better evaluate and design their strategies.

Cruise passenger spending in Puerto Rico (1960-1998)

Year	Number Cruise	Passengers Cruise	(US$mn) Spending*	(Dollars/cruise passenger) Spending
1960	105	45,337	1.5	33
1970	301	136,604	5.9	43
1980	700	505,124	20.3	40
1985	906	866,090	50.3	58
1990	911	890,348	54.4	61
1991	943	1,63,370	56.9	53
1992	850	1,014,490	65.1	64
1994	793	968,112	66.7	69
1995	740	955,105	65.6	69
1996	751	1,045,104	75.4	72
1997	674	1,105,957	84.2	76
1998	701	1,365,622	102.5	75

(*): includes crew member spending.
Source: Puerto Rico Ports Authority.

3.2.2 Sustainability of cruise tourism in SIDS

Each year cruise ships grow larger, and the list of destinations visited increases. At the same time, most cruise ships can be relatively self-contained for extended periods and therefore can have the flexibility to bring large numbers of tourists, sometimes more than 3000 passengers, with the number of disembarking passengers and crew outnumber the native residents several times over; they can bring their own water to water-short islands, take sewage to the next port with suitable treatment facilities or provide on-board treatment, and limit numbers of tourists allowed on shore at one time.

Yet, the social and environmental impacts of cruise ships can be significant, bringing both benefits and risks. The sustainability issues associated with cruise ships can be put in two categories:

- **Issues related to the operation of the ships themselves**
  - Air emissions;
  - Ballast water (containing non-native species);
  - Wastewater (sewage and grey water);
  - Hazardous wastes (photo processing fluids, dry cleaning waste fluids and contaminated materials, print shop waste fluids, fluorescent and mercury vapour lamp bulbs, anti-foulant paint, hospital wastes);
  - Solid waste (garbage - food, paper, cans, bottles, etc.);
  - Oily bilge water;
  - Effect on coral reefs.

- **Issues regarding the impacts on destinations**
  - Provision of dockside facilities for services to cruise ships,
  - Water supply;
  - Waste disposal and treatment (both liquid (sewage) and solid (garbage)
  - Impact on destination services and infrastructure;
  - Scheduling (including seasonality and multiple arrivals);
  - Crowd management;
  - Capture of benefits for the host community (revenues, jobs, capital support from cruise lines for facilities used, provisioning etc.);
  - Security (including customs and immigration controls);
  - Control of social and environmental impacts on targeted tour sites (including education of passengers);
  - Coral reefs: protection and contribution to conservation, or destruction.

Destinations often have little flexibility to influence when ships arrive or how long they stay. Where ships have very short stays, this can cause all tours to arrive at the same sites simultaneously, and also concentrate demand for other services (taxis, food, etc.) in very short periods. When ships leave before dinner, passengers wait until they are on ship to eat, reducing their spending on shore. While some lines try to coordinate with others to share berthing capacity or to stagger arrivals, destinations may have little capacity to affect the decision.

In some destinations, cruise ships will berth near shore reefs or may anchor near reefs so that passengers may take advantage of access.
Aside from economic effects, cruise activity has significant environmental effects, which are gaining prominence due to the rise in maritime traffic. Efforts are geared mainly towards preventing undesirable impacts on the natural environment, such measures include: the definition of maritime regions of special interest, limitations on the dumping of waste into the sea or requirements for the installation of less-polluting propulsion systems.

For islands that are already cruise destinations, as the Caribbean, the establishment of sustainability indicators for monitoring the impacts of cruise ships are essential. While for new destinations willing to develop or expand a burgeoning cruise industry, careful attention has to be given while evaluating the socio-economic and environmental costs; return on investment for the island economy and population's benefit (e.g. in building the necessary infrastructure, like ports or the limits of island carrying capacity). This means that cruise tourism has to be positioned as a competitor to land based tourism.

The effects generated by cruises amplify the importance of this type of holidays. The most immediate effect is the expenditure generated at destinations. Few in-depth studies have been carried out on this subject and so the available information is limited. Studies for France and the Caribbean estimate the economic impact of cruises at 87 million euros a year and 410 million dollars per semester, respectively. There is a clear need for this type of studies, as they make it possible not only to quantify the impact of the business on destinations, but also the distribution of this impact between the port community and the destination itself.

As indicated earlier, the ship is a destination in itself, and the ports of call are merely additions to the trip. This has created major competition between cruises and on-land destinations, which are backed up on both sides by aggressive advertising campaigns comparing the price of one holiday option with the other.

For destinations visited, cruises constitute a relevant primary or additional source of tourism receipts. On the one hand there is the revenue from the port services supplied, generally depending on ship tonnage and number of passengers, paid for by the cruise operators. Depending on the size and type of the port, services and supplies such as provisioning, fuel supply, maintenance and repairs also add to a lower or higher extent to the benefits. On the other hand, destinations count with the on-land tourism consumption generated by passengers and crew, related to activities such as sightseeing tours, shopping, eating and drinking, etc.

According to data about on-land activities of US and Canadian cruise passengers, over 80 per cent participate in panoramic visits, shopping and sightseeing, between 80 and 50 per cent participate in excursions, cultural visits, beach and gastronomy while about 10 per cent engage in tennis and golf. Although most cruise packages are based on full board, it is surprising to note that still over half of cruise passengers visit restaurants at the destination.

More recent figures show that on-land **expenditure in various Caribbean destinations ranged widely between US$ 15 and 270 per passenger in 2001** (CTO 2003), with the shopping offer being an important variable. Compared to over-night tourism, receipts from cruise tourism are on the whole lower, but the investment needed is also more modest.

Cruise ship spending in the Caribbean

Port	USD per Passengers (1997)
Aruba	65
Bahamas	83
Barbados	61
Curaçao	63
Grand Cayman	n/a
Key West	41
Montego Bay, Jamaica	57
Ocho Rios, Jamaica	101
San Juan	158
Saint Lucia	n/a
St. Kitts	47
St. Thomas	225
Average	**124**

Source: Florida Caribbean Cruise Association (FCCA).

If an **adequate port infrastructure is of course an absolute requisite**, however, it is not necessary to invest as heavily in air transport infrastructure or accommodation. For base ports the situation is different, as a comparatively sophisticated infrastructure is needed in order to accommodate for air arrivals and overnight stays in hotels before or after the cruise trip. Generally also more of the ship services will take place. Accordingly the economic impact will also be greater.

Chapter 4

How can tourism contribute to the sustainable development of SIDS?

As exposed in chapter 2, overcoming the challenges of sustainability for SIDS requires the introduction of **key policies and measures for mutually supportive tourism development and environmental management, taking into account the potential socio-economic local impacts as well external impacts.**

Tourism as well as any other human activity, will always produce environmental impacts, even at low levels of intensity, and despite the best efforts of governments and individuals.

Already, high population densities in many SIDS have:

- increased pressure on land resources and wildlife;
- intensified the demand for facilities to deal with waste on both land and sea;
- contributed to coastal areas being degraded, adversely affecting beaches, mangroves and coral reefs; and
- unsustainably used scarce freshwater resources.

Tourism as currently developed in some islands, often spoils the very environment on which it depends. Unsuitable large scale developments destroy mangroves and wetlands; yachts and divers can damage coral reefs, and hotels and cruise ships may discharge raw sewage into the sea. Owing to the limited land supply, tourism could lead to massive, rapid urbanization along coastal areas. Large scale commercialization may bring uncontrollable pollution and undesired overcrowding of traffic and visitors.

The tourists themselves are becoming increasingly sophisticated in their demands; this is not only in terms of luxury at the various establishments they use, but especially in terms of having a meaningful travel experience, including such aspects as cultural authenticity, contacts with local communities, and learning about flora, fauna, special ecosystems and natural life in general, and its conservation.

Integrating tourism development with sustainable island development requires the ability to bring into play some essential factors:

- **a political and operational preparedness** to support tourism on the part of the island Government;
- **a social climate** and **natural and cultural tourism resources** attractive to international tourists;
- **an international and regional accessibility** in terms of distance, time, price and adequate means of transport for the targeted tourism market;
- **the capacity of infrastructure**, quality in services and accommodation to underpin suitable expansion of tourism activities in traditional or newly established tourism centres;
- **qualified human resources**; and
- **the availability of investment capital** for island tourism development.

4.1 The balance between economic, social and environmental goals

In order to help tourism authorities and businesses in SIDS to reach sustainability levels in tourism activities, WTO has devoted particular attention to the ways in which governments could apply recommendations, within specific tourism plans or projects that can enhance sustainability in tourism and its contribution to poverty alleviation.

Sustainable tourism development, WTO Conceptual Definition 2004

Sustainable tourism development guidelines and management practices are applicable to all forms of tourism in all types of destinations, including mass tourism and the various niche tourism segments. Sustainability principles refer to the environmental, economic and socio-cultural aspects of tourism development, and a suitable balance must be established between these three dimensions to guarantee its long-term sustainability.

Thus, sustainable tourism should:

1) Make optimal use of environmental resources that constitute a key element in tourism development, maintaining essential ecological processes and helping to conserve natural heritage and biodiversity.
2) Respect the socio-cultural authenticity of host communities, conserve their built and living cultural heritage and traditional values, and contribute to inter-cultural understanding and tolerance.
3) Ensure viable, long-term economic operations, providing socio-economic benefits to all stakeholders that are fairly distributed, including stable employment and income-earning opportunities and social services to host communities, and contributing to poverty alleviation.

Sustainable tourism development requires the informed participation of all relevant stakeholders, as well as strong political leadership to ensure wide participation and consensus building. Achieving sustainable tourism is a continuous process and it requires constant monitoring of impacts, introducing the necessary preventive and/or corrective measures whenever necessary.

Sustainable tourism should also maintain a high level of tourist satisfaction and ensure a meaningful experience to the tourists, raising their awareness about sustainability issues and promoting sustainable tourism practices amongst them.

WTO conceptual definition 2004

Sustainable development is a concept that extends to a number of issues from balance in development, moderation in the use of natural resources, the importance of their renewal and the process of growth over time, to respect for the general interest and to fulfilment of mankind's basic needs, through to a fairer distribution of global financial resources.

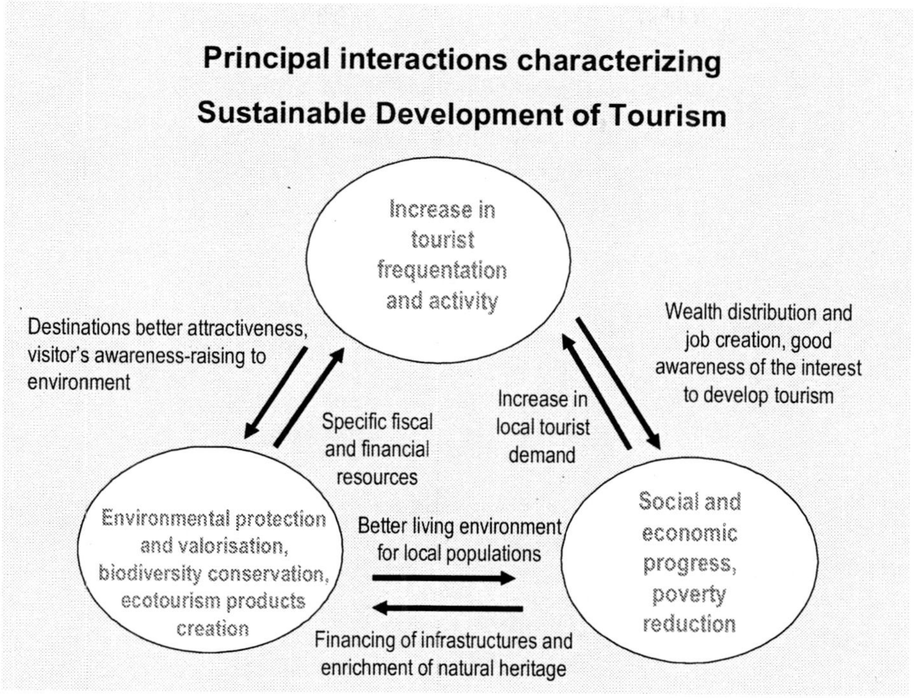

Source: WTO

In an industry as competitive as tourism, and with beach tourism forming a considerable segment, islands have been extremely active in capitalizing on the economic benefits from the development of tourism, often forgetting the potential social and environmental impacts. Experience shows that islands have also been vulnerable to mismanagement and inefficient use of their resources which, in most cases, are rare and fragile.

4.2 Recommendations and guidelines for SIDS

In 1998, the World Tourism Organization in collaboration with UNEP organized an International Conference for SIDS in Lanzarote, to examine the development of the tourism sector in SIDS and other islands and to evaluate the progress made in the implementation of the Programme of Action for the Sustainable Development of Small Island Developing States, formulated at the Barbados Conference of 1994. The challenge of sustainability in tourism development in insular territories remains as pressing as in 1998 or perhaps even more now, as consumers awareness about the environmental quality of the destinations they visit, and about the social and cultural impacts that their visits can produce, has evidently increased.

Based on the results of the Lanzarote Conference, the following guidelines have been further developed by WTO over the last couple of years:

- Tourism in SIDS should be considered as only one of the components of, and be fully **integrated into, the overall sustainable development of the island**; tourism should not replace other, traditional economic activities, but build on such activities and generate new ones, especially those in the long supply chain of tourism products and services;
- The challenges and opportunities for tourism development in SIDS for the middle and long term should be considered, and a **long term strategy** defined with a clear, commonly agreed vision;
- **Tourism planning** should be based on a sound knowledge of the natural and cultural resources of the island, aiming also at their conservation. The precondition is to undertake a detailed inventory of natural and cultural assets and their vulnerability. In particular, fragile and richly

endowed biodiversity ecosystems such as coral reefs and mangroves, and social values of the local communities should be considered. An integrated approach for the management of all resources and in particular coastal zones should be adopted.

- All stakeholders and, in particular, **local communities and the local business** sector should be involved in the definition, planning and implementation of the sustainable tourism development policy and plan, including in the establishment of carrying capacities;
- **Human resources development** should be seen as a priority in island nations; working in tourism occupations should be promoted and valued; and suitable training provided for all types of jobs;
- **SIDS should consider the environmental and socio-cultural carrying capacity** of the island in their tourism policy and strategy, and the maximum limits established in terms of both, number of tourists and built infrastructure, must be respected by all stakeholders;

  The island carrying capacity must be an essential element to be taken into consideration while planning tourism development. The carrying capacity of island systems has been defined as the degree of external impact they can assimilate without unleashing a process of deterioration. It is a central qualitative concept (not a mere quantitative formulation) to be borne in mind in drawing up a sustainable tourism scenario for the islands. It also includes maintaining a balance of tourism with other economic activities, so as to achieve an optimum outcome for sustainable development. It should be applied in a number of areas and in different ways, requiring simultaneous action on supply and demand.

  - **Environmental carrying capacity**: represents the maximum level of tourists that a particular ecosystem can absorb without risk of irreversible changes (or limits of acceptable change). If this point is exceeded, degradation of the island's ecology escalates.
  - **Socio-cultural carrying capacity**: represents the maximum number of tourists that a community is capable/willing to accept without disturbing its (traditional) social habits and way of life. If this point is exceeded, unwanted influences on the identity and cultural evolution of the island society occur.
  - **Economic carrying capacity**: represents the number of tourists/economic yield that is necessary to ensure that a destination is economically and commercially viable, but also that economic benefits remain largely locally. If this point is not reached, both tourism and other strategic sectors in the island's economic system are adversely affected.
  - **Psychological carrying capacity**: represents the maximum number of tourists that each individual visitor is prepared to accept at a destination. If this point is exceeded, tourist satisfaction begins to decline, and with it, a deterioration of the island's image and its long term commercial sustainability.

- Sustainable tourism in SIDS requires the development and adoption of **alternative building designs** of tourism facilities, according to the characteristics of each island and with a view to ensuring a sustainable use of their natural resources; in this respect, there is ample room for the private sector to exercise its creativity and imagination, while at the same time attracting more sophisticated layers of consumers looking for authenticity and differentiation;
- **Development and adoption of ecoefficiency** and cleaner production strategies and policies are also required; in particular, the use of renewable energy sources and environmentally sound technologies should be considered in all building construction tourism projects;

- **Voluntary codes of conduct**, industry standards and ecolabels should be adapted and tailored to suit particularities of SIDS; governments should encourage the adoption by the business sector of such standards and eco-certificates, providing financial or other incentives, but exercising at the same time adequate supervision of their fulfilment;
- **All stakeholders and local communities should be involved in tourism development and management and reap benefits from tourism.** Public and private partnerships should be considered not only for the development but also the rehabilitation of tourism facilities and services;
- **Environmental management systems** in hotels and other tourism establishments should be adopted as a normal practice in order to constantly gauge environmental performance, avoid over-consumption of scarce resources, attempt cost savings and reduce waste, which is always difficult to dispose of in small islands. Various alternative design techniques are available; however, they have to be adequately promoted and resources need to be made available, as well as fiscal incentives for Environmental Management System for hotels and other tourism operations.
- **Monitoring of impacts** is a necessary condition for sustainable development. It is even more important in SIDS given the characteristics of their natural and cultural environment. It is thus essential that SIDS identify and develop sets of indicators for assessing the sustainability of tourism in their island destinations, ideally establishing tourism observatories;
- **Indicators** must respond to areas of risk and vulnerability of SIDS: environmental, social and economic fields. The process of identifying the most suitable indicators for each island destination should be participatory, involving all stakeholders, especially all institutions involved in environmental protection and conservation.

4.3 Sustainability indicators for tourism

Sustainability indicators play a fundamental role in overall destination planning and management, and are an integral element in efforts to promote the sustainable development of the tourism sector, at all destinations and scales. The stimulus for the use of indicators in the tourism sector comes from the perception that many destinations have been at risk due to insufficient attention to the impacts of tourism and to the long-term sustainability of destinations. Incidences of contaminated beaches and damaged cultural and ecological assets, hostile reactions to tourists and to tourism development, and resultant problems for the tourism sector have occurred in many regions.

Tourism cannot be planned or managed in isolation from the environments, economies and communities that are part of the destination. Indicators are therefore shared with other stakeholders (ministries, local authorities, private and non-governmental organizations) that have specific mandates, for example, for environmental protection, infrastructure development or social well being. Indicators are also shared with other agencies such as the jurisdictions that are the sources of tourists for the destination, tour operators and transportation companies which bring them to the destinations or nearby destinations that may be part of a tourism experience.

Extensive studies have led WTO to prepare a guidebook, **published in 2004, *Indicators for Sustainable Development for Tourism Destinations***, providing destinations and small island nations with practical tools for developing and managing tourism in a sustainable way. The use of the indicators guidebook will be a very valuable asset for all tourism stakeholders in destinations.

A broad understanding of the need to establish and use indicators is essential for any island destination.

Types of Indicators:

- **Early warning indicators** (e.g. decline in numbers of tourists who intend to return);
- **Indicators of stresses on the system** (e.g., water shortages, or crime indices);
- **Measures of the current state** of tourism industry (e.g., occupancy rate, tourist satisfaction);
- **Measures of the impact** of tourism development on the biophysical and socio-economic environments (e.g. Indices of the level of deforestation, changes of consumption patterns and income levels in local communities);
- **Measures of management effort** (e.g., cleanup cost for coastal contamination);
- **Measures of management effect,** results or performance (e.g., changed pollution levels, greater number of returning tourists).

While all categories of indicators can be valuable in supporting sustainable tourism, **the early warning indicators** are frequently most useful to tourism managers and may provide the ability to anticipate serious negative effects on the island nation, or on the overall tourist experience. Ideally, indicators can enable actions to be taken *well before* serious threats to sustainability occur. It should also be noted that the same indicator can frequently serve different purposes and its use can change over time (e.g. an indicator of *stresses on the system* will serve later on to measure the *effects and results of management* efforts taken in response to the problems identified, becoming in effect, a performance measure for the response).

It needs to be emphasized that indicators are not an end in themselves. They become relevant only if used in tourism planning and management processes, and ideally they become effective in creating better and more sustainable decisions.

Building good and responsive indicators is not enough; it is but the first step in making a difference. The real desired outcomes lie in the creation of sustainable destinations; indicators can be significant and strategic building blocks in this process.

Indicators provide the means for continuously checking and refining integrated planning and management activity. Indicators are not only desirable in planning: **they are essential**, at least in the following planning stages:

a. **Defining values:** The foundations of planning are values, tangible and intangible expression of what is most important to people. Individual and community values are used as a kind of touchstone to all planning activity. But most people are unfamiliar with describing their values precisely, and may need to use generalizations that mean different things to different people. **Indicators become the vehicle for turning subjective values into objective and therefore specific (often quantified) measures.**

   For example, many tourists place a value on an island destination being "uncrowded". But to what extent is a place considered "uncrowded" is perceived differently by different host communities and tourists of different origins and ages. For planners who wish to act to maintain satisfaction levels regarding crowding, an indicator measuring the actual number of people in a given area, monitoring the time it takes to be served, or calculating what percentage of the tourists or locals believe that it is "crowded" is needed; precisely how many people is too many, or what are the limits to acceptable crowding? Clarification of these values can lead to agreement on acceptable use levels and perhaps direct the actions needed to achieve them.

b. **Defining desired outcomes:** Desired outcomes are a common second level to planning which try to convert the values of society or stakeholders into a desirable situation or condition that is more accessible and which can lead to definable actions. Indicators force greater clarity in definition of what is desired. **Over a plan or program period, the indicator becomes the key measurement for progress.**

Examples of broad social values which are important to sustainable tourism include:

- conserving the natural environment;
- satisfied tourists;
- viable tourism businesses; and
- a content host community.

If the broad goal is "conservation of the natural environment", then an assessment could show for example that only 10% of the local environment is protected, and that over 20% has notable ecological value as habitat. With this indicator as a basis, an objective of 18% protected within 5 years could be established. This is a measurable objective with a specific time target.

c. **Defining objectives, strategies and actions:** After the desired outcomes have been established (often expressed as specific targets relative to the objectives), planning then focuses on how they may best be achieved. The result normally includes a range of objectives, of strategies to achieve them and actions which support the strategies. Constraints may also exist, which need to be monitored. This often shows the need for additional indicators in the planning process to help in the clear measurement of constraints.

   Some constraints may be difficult to describe: Will the island community oppose a high density of development?, or will labour be available to carry out the project when needed? Indicators can also be important to clarify risks and areas which require attention in the planning process. For example, an indicator helping to measure a dwindling wildlife population can trigger specific actions to protect, manage, or close a site as part of the plan.

d. **Choosing between alternatives:** Often there are alternative courses of strategies and actions to choose between. Choosing is not easy when there is a lack of information about the current situation, let alone the potential strengths and benefits of each alternative. Indicators can be important to gain a cost effective idea of these situations.

   For example, a planner trying to choose between proposals permitting either a 50 bed or a 100 bed accommodation to proceed. If the planner is concerned about the respective water use, he/she could seek out the average amount of water used per room in similar establishments, and compare the alternative amounts with the known sustainable supply in the local area. The same indicators will act as performance measures regarding the degree to which plans and actions respond to the issue. Ideally, indicators are already in use which can be obtained by each proponent and used to guide proposals. An interesting use of indicators as key inputs into a geographical information system (GIS) is being developed to integrate tourism demand and supply scenarios in the Cayman Islands, where a spatial approach tries to reconcile a range of demands with the known ecological sensitivities of the destination.

e. **Checking performance:** After a plan has been completed, its implementation begins. Planners need to know which actions and strategies are the most effective - so they can channel resources to successful approaches and re-work unsuccessful ones.

   Often the implementation can take years, but the planner needs to know, before the end of the planning period, what is working and what isn't. Indicators are extremely useful at testing the success of a plan as it is being implemented, because indicators are able to efficiently sample a situation to determine if changes have occurred. For example, a plan seeking to increase tourism might sample the number of operators or the number of jobs directly attributable to tourism.

f. **Revise desired outcomes:** After checking performance, indicators will sometimes suggest that a plan may need to be changed because the key factors affecting the destination or its tourism have changed. Sometimes plans must change because the development occurred more quickly than expected, and to continue with the original planned activities might create a problem. Indicators, used over the course of planned activity, **provide valuable direction for considering how to alter a strategy** or action in a way that is most likely to improve the situation to become closer to the desired outcome.

   For example, in order to stimulate tourism business, the plan might have permitted access to a sensitive area. An indicator could have determined that instead of taking two years, the level of use or activity was achieved in six months, and that further stimulation would be unsustainable. The plan could, based on this new information, be changed from stimulation to management of the new activity and businesses.

g. **Create a learning environment:** Some people think that planning is the responsibility only of professional planners. This is an unreasonable assumption, as good planning needs a diversity of input and often also needs additional participation and partnership to be effective. Indicators provide a way to **involve a wider range of participants in the strategic planning process.**

The newly released WTO Guidebook on Indicators of Sustainable Development for Tourism Destinations includes a case study on a Caribbean regional initiative. It shows how the Caribbean is progressing towards a common set of indicators to be shared among destinations, and what are the specific indicators needed for most small island states.

The Caribbean Sustainable Tourism Indicators Initiative Regional Indicators, Methods of Definition, Standards

The Sustainable Tourism Zone of the Caribbean (STZC) was officially created by the signature of the Convention for Sustainable Tourism, in 2001 during the Third Summit of the Association of Caribbean States (ACS). The objective of this Convention is to establish that the Zone is a geographically determined cultural, socio-economic and biologically rich and diverse unit, in which tourism development will depend on sustainability and the principles of integration, cooperation and consensus, aimed at facilitating the integrated development of the Greater Caribbean.

The STZC is a framework to promote sustainable tourism policies and practices in Caribbean tourism destinations, and fostering community participation in decision-making, planning and in general, in the benefits and solutions to problems generated by tourism activity.

The strategy for facing this challenge involves the two main actors: the States as agents of management and change, and the civil society as a new emerging actor, in the era of globalization. Several steps have been taken toward the achievement of the STZC objectives, including the elaboration of a guide for piloting sustainable tourism in specific sites and businesses, through an action agenda and the development of sustainability indicators which will be adapted to the specific characteristics of the Greater Caribbean Region.

The initial indicators work was developed in 2002 by the French Agency for Tourist Engineering (AFIT) and the French Consulting Geo-System. The working methodology was based on an analysis of tourism in the Caribbean, a proposal for adapting the AFIT method to the context of the Caribbean on the basis of a pilot project in a test area and a trial of the method at Saint François in Guadeloupe. Based on the AFIT Report ACS elaborated a **Manual of Procedures for Trainers in Sustainable Tourism,** in order to facilitate the practical application of sustainable tourism indicators and planning processes at destinations.

The Manual contains the following parts:

1. **Sustainable tourism in the Caribbean**: includes the concept of sustainable tourism and its implications for the development of destinations, the role of stakeholders, and examples on awareness-raising activities.
2. **How to pilot sustainable tourism in destinations**: a procedure for analyzing sustainability issues, defining strategies and action plans and monitoring through indicators.
3. **Indicators and sustainability: contains the detailed description of sustainable tourism indicators** proposed for the Greater Caribbean, together with methods for measurement, examples of good practices and standards where they exist.

A dual system of indicators is proposed, considering common regional aspects and specific needs of the different territories and destinations:

- Global, or normative indicators, which take into account the common elements for the group of territories of the ACS;
- Custom indicators, which respond to specific needs of local tourism destinations.

The indicators are grouped according to four dimensions of sustainability: heritage, economy, social, ethical.

Normative indicators for Caribbean destinations

The Caribbean initiative is an attempt to create a tool which both responds to local and national needs for each member but also permits some exchange of information and coordination at a regional scale. This case shows the initial steps in creating the process and some of the indicators, which will be the basis for common collection and use. The **14 normative indicators** defined refer to basic sustainability issues, such as the management of natural resources (energy, water, waste, environmental conservation), preservation of local culture, safety, benefits to the local economy (integration of local businesses, employment), tourist satisfaction, among others.

In the Greater Caribbean, the main difficulty in indicators application is obtaining reliable data to reflect the diversity of the parties involved and the businesses. In addition, even if these data exist, it is very difficult, if not impossible, to compare them, as they differ immensely from State to State. The second difficulty lies in the actual content of these data, which only take into account businesses which have a legal existence. In the Caribbean, the informal economy has a very important place in the tourism sector: illicit street sellers of handicrafts, take-away food, alternative accommodation with no legal status, street guides, etc. Nevertheless, use of the existing data is vital as long as its relevance is systematically determined. In all cases, the destinations must mobilize their own resources, using their own know-how and innovation to solve this problem.

The first application of the ACS manual on indicators took place during the **First Caribbean Workshop on Sustainable Tourism Indicators**, in Trinidad and Tobago, October 2004. The workshop was organized jointly with the World Tourism Organization, and followed the WTO training methodology which is based on a case study destination, demonstrating the work with indicators in a real situation, with the involvement of local stakeholders. The case study area, the Chaguaramas Peninsula in the island of Trinidad, served as a pilot project to test the ACS indicators, and with some important lessons on the complexity of indicators application and the need for processes tailored to the specific characteristics of each destination. The consolidation of a Caribbean indicators framework will be a gradual process, based on the experiences that will be drawn from a series of upcoming pilot projects and further workshops at local destinations.

Sources:
Indicators of Sustainable Development for Tourism Destinations – A Guidebook (WTO, 2004)
Final Report: Caribbean Workshop on Sustainable Tourism Indicators, Trinidad and Tobago, October 2004

Indicators provide a reality check, forcing planners to be precise, to define in real terms what they are using as targets, what specific actions are intended, and what the desired goals or outcomes really mean: not just cleaner water, but how much cleaner, when, how much better than now, and at what cost; not just "more tourists" but how many, when, where, and bringing what benefits to the local economy. Indicators stimulate discussion, and may lead to debate, or to consensus.

The development of a means of monitoring the health of tourism and other key values in destinations involves a wide range of groups and can result in more coordinated and supportive approaches to sustainable tourism.

Indicators can provide a level of specificity that is often lacking in plans that must deal with complex issues. In this way, indicators provide people with the opportunity to understand every part of the planning process, and how to be involved. Indicators are also extremely valuable at monitoring the progress of a plan's implementation to check on its success and identify whether parts of the plan should be altered. **These uses increase the level of participation in planning and subsequently add valuable insights and expertise and improve the use of scarce resources like in SIDS.**

There are various international initiatives that provide the rationale for indicators of sustainable development and also suggest particular measures which may be of use at many scales. These include:

The UN Commission on Sustainable Development has developed a Theme Indicator Framework, which addresses overall sustainability issues, with specific subsets that may be directly applicable to tourism destinations or to key assets. It also defined guidelines for developing a national indicator programmes.
http://www.un.org/esa/sustdev/natlinfo/indicators/isd.htm

The Global Reporting Initiative (GRI) attempts to set world standards on environmental reporting for public and private organizations. http://www.globalreporting.org/

Based on GRI, the *Tour Operators Initiative* has elaborated guidelines for sustainability reporting through performance indicators for tour operators. http://www.toinitiative.org/

4.4 Certification systems

Credible and transparent certification programs provide a tool to reward tourism operations that employ "best practices" and to differentiate them from less environmentally and socially responsible endeavours.

Through voluntary, independently assessed sustainable tourism and ecotourism certification programs, tourism businesses, attractions, and activities can demonstrate commitment towards conserving biodiversity and fostering social well being. Certification programs can also provide businesses with guidelines for improving their environmental and social performance.

Certification of sustainable tourism can help to reduce the negative environmental and social impacts of tourism, ensure that the tourism industry is held accountable and provide marketing benefits to those firms that meet the certification standards.

Certification systems for sustainable tourism need to be developed and operated to fit geographical, political, socio-economic and sectoral characteristics of each country. For this reason, the recommendations issued by WTO[3] serve as general orientation and they need to be adapted to the economic, institutional, social and environmental conditions prevailing in each island state.

A WTO study on voluntary initiatives for sustainable tourism revealed that governments have an important role in many of the certification systems presently operating. Government involvement can be either through direct financial support, marketing support, expert know-how in criteria setting, verification procedures, or surveillance of procedures followed by the certification body. Government agencies involved generally include either environment ministries, national tourism authorities and tourist boards, and in fewer cases, standards institutes.

Certification systems can bring benefits to society, the environment, governments, private companies and consumers as well.

• Potential benefits for society

Generally speaking, societies will benefit from certification systems that cover the three aspects of sustainability: social, environmental and economic. Certified companies are supposed to generate benefits in these three areas, while reducing their negative impacts. Therefore, the contribution of tourism activities to the sustainable development of host societies will be more evident, more measurable and more accountable.
Furthermore, the level of awareness on sustainability issues will be stronger in the host society if the large majority of tourism companies and/or destinations are certified.

• Potential benefits for the environment

It is evident that certification systems and ecolabels that include strict environmental criteria result in benefits for the local environment and, to the extent that some mass tourism activities can impact biodiversity and climate change, also the global environment.

Furthermore, the widespread use of ecolabels and certification systems in the tourism industry helps to generate increased environmental awareness among both, tourists and host societies and should result in more caring attitudes with respect to the natural and built environments.

• Potential benefits for governments:

- Providing an effective alternative to direct regulation, which could prove more difficult and time-consuming to implement;
- Enabling governments to adopt a flexible approach to monitoring the tourism industry, permitting organizations to proceed at the pace they feel most comfortable with, while

3 WTO recommendations to governments for supporting and/or establishing national certification systems for sustainable tourism, World Tourism Organization, 2003
http://www.world-tourism.org/sustainable/doc/certification-gov-recomm.pdf

encouraging them to develop innovative approaches to environmental and socio-cultural improvements;

- Giving tourism companies greater scope for making environmental and social improvements by exploiting opportunities specific to their individual circumstances, rather than governments having to control and inspect companies in order to check that they comply with general, industry-wide regulations;
- Allowing part of the costs of implementing and monitoring environmental protection measures to be transferred to the industry itself, thereby reducing the financial burden of regulation on the taxpayer;
- National programs of tourism certification can enhance tourism's recognition in the country, national competitiveness and image in international markets.

- **Potential benefits for companies:**

  - Adherence to voluntary environmental initiatives can enable the company to market its products more effectively, and to improve their public image among consumers, business partners and with the host communities;
  - Engaging in voluntary certification can help companies to signal their specific commitment to environmental, social and even economic improvements, which may in turn help to defer the need for further direct regulation by governments;
  - Participation in a certification programme can provide better access to modern techniques, technology and know-how;
  - Applying effective environmental management can help to protect the environmental and cultural assets upon which the tourism industry depends for its continued prosperity.
  - Pursuing sound environmental management strategies can generate substantial cost savings for the company.

Finally, certification and ecolabels can **benefit consumers** by providing them with more information and guidance for their decisions on travel choices, as well as assurances for product and service quality.

4.5 Partnerships, a key tool for creating a conducive environment for the sustainable development of tourism

Many Small Island Developing States have established initiatives to balance tourism activities with broader economic, social and environmental objectives at the regional, national and local levels. In particular, major efforts have led to:

a) the strengthening of regional cooperation on strategies, standards and capacity-building for tourism,

b) the assistance of international institutions, the private sector and nongovernmental organizations in the area of human and institutional capacity-building,

c) the formulation of integrated national action plans, strategies and policies for tourism and environmental protection, and

d) the establishment of frameworks that allow local communities to participate and have greater control over tourism development in their localities.

Role of the major stakeholders for Sustainable Tourism Development:

- **At local level:** as the **size and scarcity of resources** are characteristic of SIDS, the cooperation between;
  - the **Government** (Tourism, Transport, Finance, Environment, Culture, Land use, Employment, Education, Industry);
  - the **private sector** (all tourism operators, airlines, cruise lines, DMO's, travel agencies, service providers, craft, supply industries, port facilities, cargo, etc.) and
  - the **Civil Society** (NGO's in conservation, research, culture, arts, craft...) from the country or archipelago;

  It is essential to create a critical mass of resources and a sufficient scale for any development or action, as well as to define an appropriate framework for responsible development of tourism in the island nation.

- **At regional level:** as **the isolation** is a key issue in most SIDS, all policies and measures that could benefit from economies of scale should be dealt with within networks and regional organizations at all levels (Government, Private enterprise, NGO, etc.). The example of the Caribbean Tourism Organization is important to mention, as it has placed this part of the world in the mind of people and its islands as the "Caribbean".

  Regional cooperation is an important tool for the sustainable development of tourism in SIDS. In particular:
  - environmental regulations and standards should be harmonized for SIDS in the same region;
  - voluntary industry codes, standards and ecolabels should also be considered, whenever possible, at the regional level;
  - exchange of experiences and dissemination of good practices in tourism, from the social, environmental and economic points of view, should be stimulated among SIDS of the same region;
  - awareness raising campaigns on tourism-related issues and capacity building activities should be launched at the regional level whenever possible;
  - SIDS could consider joining forces for facilitating the funding of sustainable tourism projects and activities.

  Regional and international organizations should encourage and assist in this regional cooperation.

- **At international level: "think globally, act locally"** should be the streamline of SIDS commitment in sustainable tourism development. A lot has to be gained in sharing experience, know how and guidance from the international community. As for other sectors as Industry, Agriculture, Manufacturing, Tourism is to be recognized as a powerful tool for sustainable development of SIDS.

  International organizations, and in particular WTO in collaboration with other UN Agencies, could :
  - assist with the development and implementation of :
    a. transfer of technology and know-how and more widely with sustainable development approaches in the tourism sector;
    b. voluntary approaches such as codes of conduct and ecolabels;
    c. indicators of sustainability in tourism;
    d. develop exchange of experiences at the international level on sustainable tourism in SIDS;
  - disseminate existing pilot projects and good practices;

- develop or participate in awareness raising campaigns and capacity building activities for sustainable tourism;
- establish an international observatory for monitoring the sustainability of tourism in SIDS.

The World Summit on Sustainable Development, in 2002, agreed in paragraph 43 of the Johannesburg Plan of Implementation to call for *"Enhancing (tourism) international cooperation, foreign direct investment and partnerships with both private and public sectors, at all levels."* It is only through effective regional and international cooperation that the complexity of sustainable tourism development will be possible.

Chapter 5

WTO: a small agency with a large mission

The World Tourism Organization has been recognized since December 2003 as the new UN specialized agency responsible for tourism. This new status in the UN will help to strengthen the close and continuous coordination among the different agencies of the United Nations system, as well as other relevant organizations dealing with sustainability issues as they affect tourism.

WTO has been producing know-how and specific guidelines for the sustainable development and management of tourism in different types of destinations. It has also been disseminating good practices observed throughout the world, and supporting governments and the private sector with the necessary tools and technical advice to continuously raise the level of sustainability of the industry.

The World Tourism Organization has been assisting developing countries to strengthen their national and local economies through tourism development since its foundation in 1975. The integration of the Millennium Development Goals in what is today a pivotal sector of the world economy, as well as the reduction of poverty through the sustainable development of tourism have become a central issue in the work of the Organization.

As the leading international organization in the field of travel and tourism, the World Tourism Organization (WTO) is vested by the United Nations with a central and decisive role in promoting the development of responsible, sustainable and universally accessible tourism, with the aim of contributing to economic development, international understanding, peace, prosperity and universal respect for, and observance of, human rights and fundamental freedoms. In pursuing this aim, the Organization pays particular attention to the interests of the developing countries in the field of tourism.

Acting as an umbrella organization for world tourism, WTO plays a catalytic role in promoting technology transfers and international cooperation, in stimulating and developing public-private sector partnerships and in encouraging the implementation of the Global Code of Ethics for Tourism, with a view to ensuring that member countries, tourist destinations and businesses maximize the positive economic, social and cultural effects of tourism and fully reap its benefits, while at the same time they minimize its negative social and environmental impacts.

Through tourism, WTO aims at stimulating economic growth and job creation, providing incentives for protecting the environment and cultural heritage, and promoting peace, prosperity and respect for human rights.

• Global Code of Ethics

Adopted by the WTO General Assembly in 1999 and acknowledged by the United Nations General Assembly in 2001 by a special resolution, the Code sets out a ten point blueprint for safeguarding the resources upon which tourism depends and ensuring that its economic benefits are equitably shared. They are included in the paragraph 43 of the JPoI of the World Summit on Sustainable Development.

The Code is based on the principles of sustainability that underpin all WTO's programmes, with special emphasis on involving local communities in planning, managing and monitoring tourism development. It includes nine articles outlining the "rules of the game" for destinations, governments, tour operators, travel agents, tourism workers and developers, and travellers themselves. The tenth article involves implementation of the code through the activities of the World Committee on Tourism Ethics.

The **Global Code of Ethics for Tourism** spells out, in a balanced way:

- the **rights and obligations** of the various partners that together make up the tourism industry;
- the symmetrical and complementary **rules incumbent** on those that **visit and those that receive;**
- a reflection of shared values, but also a source of **normative guidance** for the many stakeholders whose involvement is crucial if tourism is to evolve in a way that benefits all;
- a help to **minimize the negative impact** of tourism on the environment and on cultural heritage;
- a help to **maximize the benefits** for residents as well as for visitors.

• Rio Earth Summit - 1992

Since the Rio Earth Summit, sustainability has become the central issue in tourism development policies throughout the world. Although the World Tourism Organization had been promoting environmentally friendly and culturally sensitive tourism policies, including methodological approaches for implementation since the mid-1980s, the Rio Summit clearly meant a turning point in the level of awareness about sustainable practices in tourism among governments and major groups. ces in tourism among governments and major groups.

• Agenda 21 for the Travel and Tourism Industry - 1995

The World Tourism Organization, jointly with the World Travel and Tourism Council, formulated an Agenda 21 follow-up for the Travel and Tourism Industry in 1995, being the only economic sector to have used the global Agenda 21 - emanating from the Rio Earth Summit - to develop its own agenda for action.

Agenda 21 specifies actions that industry can take to bring about sustainable development and ways in which governments can facilitate this process. The Agenda 21 for the Travel and Tourism Industry, aims to help government departments with responsibility for tourism, national tourism administrations (NTA's), representative trade organizations and travel and tourism companies fulfil their potential to achieve sustainable development at local and national levels.

• WTO International Conference on Sustainable Tourism in Small Island Developing States (SIDS) and Other Islands - 1998

The conference was held in **Lanzarote**, Spain in October 1998 jointly by the World Tourism Organization (WTO) and the United Nations Environment Programme (UNEP). The Lanzarote Conference examined the development of the tourism sector in SIDS. Among many discussions and conclusions, the main issue was how to develop tourism in small islands, which are fragile, vulnerable and sensitive to tourists influx, and, at the same time, have rich biodiversity to offer to tourists, in a sustainable manner.

• UN-CSD 7 - 1999

The UN Commission on Sustainable Development also took an interest in the tourism sector and the need for it to be developed in a sustainable manner. At its 7th session (April 1999), it focused on tourism, made a number of recommendations to governments and to the private tourism sector, and took a number of decisions in this respect.

- **WTO International Seminar on Sustainable Tourism and Competitiveness in the Islands of the Mediterranean - 2000**

Held in **Capri**, Italy in May 2000, the conference was about tourism in the Mediterranean islands. Still, many findings can be shared by many islands in other regions. The focal point of the conference was the growing relationship between tourism competitiveness and sustainability, and some of the challenges of tourism supply in the islands of the Mediterranean were examined.

- **WTO International Conference on Sustainable Tourism in the Islands of the Asia-Pacific Regions - 2000**

The conference was held in December 2000 in **Hainan**, China, as a follow-up to the previous conferences. The aim of the Conference was to examine the various aspects that need to be considered by governments and the private sector if they wish tourism to contribute to the overall economic, social and environmental sustainability of their territories. The conference emphasized that sustainable tourism in Asia-Pacific islands requires effective partnerships between stakeholders - the governments, tourism industry, landholders and land managers, and local communities.

- **WTO International Conference on Sustainable Tourism and Island Economies - 2001**

This was the fourth WTO Conference on Island Tourism, and was held in **Jeju**, Republic of Korea in June 2001. The Conference focused on economic aspects with emphasis on the sustainable management of tourism. Hence, the prime goal of the conference was to share information and expertise as relate to economic impact of tourism, strategies to enhance economic benefits and reduce costs; trends in island tourism, marketing and investment strategies.

- **World Summit on Sustainable Development - 2002**

The World Summit on Sustainable Development (WSSD) was a useful step for many issues in relation with sustainability. In the field of tourism, substantive progress was made in comparison with Rio, where tourism was not dealt with. In the Plan of Implementation of Johannesburg, references to tourism can be found in relation with energy, biodiversity conservation, Small Island Developing States and African issues, and a complete article on tourism was included.

- **The International Year of Ecotourism - 2002**

The United Nations declared the year 2002 as the International Year of Ecotourism. WTO organized ten preparatory conferences and the World Ecotourism Summit (Québec, May 2002). A specific conference on ecotourism for SIDS took place in Seychelles.

- **WTO Publications and Activities related to SDT**

In order to help tourism authorities and entrepreneurs to reach higher levels of sustainability in tourism activities, WTO has produced various publications, the most important of which are:

- **Guide for Local Authorities on Developing Sustainable Tourism**
  This guide presents concepts, principles, and techniques for planning and developing tourism and includes sections on managing environmental and socio-economic impacts at the local level. It is mainly intended for local authorities, whose responsibility in shaping tourism development is increasing; it also helps private developers and managers. Supplementary volumes of this Guide are available for Sub-Saharan Africa, Asia and the Pacific and Latin America and the Caribbean, containing numerous examples of application of sustainability principles in these regions.

- **Indicators of Sustainable Tourism**
  After a first book published in 1996, the World Tourism Organization released in 2004 a revised guide on the use of sustainability indicators in tourism development. The new study is based on a comprehensive international review of experiences on this subject. The issues and destination sections are illustrated with specific examples and 17 case studies from all continents.

- **Guidelines: Development of National Parks and Protected Areas for Tourism**
  Sustainable development requires part of the earth's land area to be set aside as protected areas. In order to assist countries and park managers to achieve a sustainable tourism use of their National Parks and related protected areas, WTO and UNEP have joined forces with the World Conservation Union (IUCN) to publish these guidelines in a new, enlarged and updated version published in 2002.

- **Sustainable Development of Tourism – A Compilation of Good Practices**
  The progress towards a more sustainable tourism industry is best demonstrated through success stories. Three publications, one on sustainable tourism and two more specifically on ecotourism contain more than 150 examples of good practices collected worldwide. A great variety of projects are presented, ranging from local to regional and national levels, including activities of the public, private and NGO sectors, covering aspects of eco-, rural- and cultural tourism, accommodations, tour operations, transportation, protected area management, regulatory and voluntary frameworks, among others.

- **Ecotourism Market Studies**
  On the occasion of the International Year of Ecotourism, WTO prepared a series of market reports with the aim to increase the knowledge of seven important country markets: Canada, France, Germany, Italy, Spain, United Kingdom and the United States of America. These publications are a precious help for ecotourism inbound operators in natural destinations to develop their activities.

- **Tourism and Climate Change**
  WTO organized in 2003 in Djerba, Tunisia, the first event on this theme. The proceedings of the Djerba Conference highlighted islands as one of the most threatened tourism destinations, due among others, to see level rise.

- **Manual for Congestion management in tourism sites**
  This WTO study is of great value to local authorities, as many islands are facing increasing problems with the congestion created by large numbers of visitors. It provides guidelines,

practical tools and case study examples for congested sites from the demand-, destination- and site-management perspectives.

- **Tourism and World Heritage Sites**
  For tourism promoters World Heritage Sites act as magnets, while for the nation in which they are found they serve as icons that continue to influence current values. This handbook concentrates on human-made sites. It is devoted to helping the managers of World Heritage Sites accomplish a dual purpose: to conserve the site given to their care and provide meaningful and considerate access to as many visitors as the site can allow.

• Sustainable Tourism and Poverty Reduction

A first publication on **Tourism and Poverty Alleviation** was launched at the World Summit on Sustainable Development (Johannesburg) in 2002. It provided a comprehensive analysis on tourism's contribution to the alleviation of poverty in developing and least developed countries and defined some principal areas of action.

A second publication in this series was presented at ITB, Berlin in March 2004. This new volume, titled **"Tourism and Poverty Alleviation: Recommendations for Action"**, defines practical approaches to involve poor layers of the society in tourism operations and make sure that tourism development projects generate direct and indirect benefits to them.

A WTO newly launched programme, Sustainable Tourism for Eliminating Poverty: ST-EP focuses on longstanding work to encourage sustainable tourism - social, economic and ecological - which specifically alleviates poverty, bringing development and jobs to people living on less than a dollar a day. It targets the world's poorest countries, particularly in Africa and developing states in general, including SIDS.

In the framework of the ST-EP initiative, WTO is working with partners on research and practical action to identify the most effective ways in which tourism can be used towards the alleviation of poverty.

WTO will be in a position to start ST-EP operations during 2005. The Korean Government has committed US$ 5 million over the next 4 years to ST-EP, plus covering all the administrative costs of a ST-EP Foundation in Seoul, the Dutch government contributed with 2 million euro to a ST-EP Technical Assistance Trust Fund and the Dutch Cooperation Agency SNV is already contributing in kind. WTO is currently fielding exploratory missions to a number of countries including small islands nations, in order to identify ST-EP projects, so that when the Foundation and the funds are in place, a project portfolio for immediate action will be ready.

• Promoting public – private sector partnerships – WTOBC

WTO is unique among international intergovernmental organizations in that it is open to membership by the operational sector and promotes various methods of cooperation amongst its Members. Airlines, hotel chains, tour operators, trade associations, consultants, promotion boards and educational institutions make up the approximately 350 Members of the WTO Business Council (WTOBC).

WTOBC utilizes a partnership approach to tourism as a method to promote public and private integration and as a model of increased understanding between the two sectors. To achieve their objectives, WTOBC aids Members in expanding their tourism businesses through industry networking, forming contacts with the necessary government officials, strengthening industry-education relationship, and conducting specialized research projects for the private sector.

The WTOBC is undertaking numerous projects with the aim of creating more public-private partnerships and sustained cooperation amongst tourism industries. These projects include investigations into the factors that affect tourism, methods of managing congestion on sites, assisting small and medium size enterprises, and implementing new technologies.

Under the guidance of its Board of Directors, WTOBC complements its research with annual studies, data compilation, research publication and organization of conferences. The Council promotes integration between public and private sectors with themes that are of special interest to the business community.

• Building awareness on the importance of tourism

Governments have been putting higher priority on tourism during recent crises. WTO's website on the Internet (www.world-tourism.org), available in English, French and Spanish, supports governments in such efforts. The homepage offers the latest news from WTO and easy-to-use links to all activities and products. Users have access to basic statistics on world tourism, seminar programmes and a complete calendar of worldwide tourism events.

With the introduction of the **e-library**, special accessibility to WTO Members has been given for a comprehensive access to all research papers, statistics, publications and internal working documents.

• "Tourism enriches individuals, families, communities and all the world."

During the first World Conference on Tourism Communications (TOURCOM), held in early 2004, WTO launched a world public awareness campaign about the importance of tourism. The campaign is a powerful tool to promote tourism at all levels of society. Recommendations in most WTO conferences organized for Small Island Developing States highlight the importance of awareness building among local communities as well as individuals for achieving a sustainable development. This aspect has not been yet fully implemented and this campaign could be a powerful response.

The aims of the **Tourism enriches campaign** are:

- to promote tourism as a basic human right and way of life, which enriches individuals, family, societies and nations;
- to stimulate communication about the benefits of tourism as the most prospective economic activity for the local communities and countries;
- to enhance cooperation between destinations and the tourism industry with the local, regional and international media;
- to link individual tourism entities to the larger community of international tourism.

Successful sustainable tourism in SIDS will require a good understanding of the socio-economic impacts it can bring to the country, through a change in mentality of all stakeholders in tourism development and management. It is thus essential that awareness campaigns and educational programmes be developed to reach the various stakeholders.

Conclusion

Since 1998 in Lanzarote, there is growing evidence that various measures are being developed in SIDS and other islands in order to improve the integration of tourism in sustainable island development. Nonetheless, progress towards sustainable tourism is slow, while inter-island cooperation and information are still weak. Therefore, a new level of commitment should be considered for encouraging sustainable tourism development in small island nations.

Ever since the leading international fora decided it was necessary to lay down a new groundwork for addressing the viability of development, a series of key criteria and concepts concerning the interrelationship between tourism, the environment, and sustainability have been formulated, in turn necessitating the reformulation of many parameters and new procedures in use today.

Islands differ greatly in size, climate, terrain, biodiversity, access, human history, habitation, culture, land tenure, legal systems and economic activity, including tourism. Due to their relatively small size, islands are vulnerable from both an environmental and a socio-economic point of view. During the last decade tourism, as a major export industry, has increased its economic contribution in most of small island nations, compared with other sectors as agriculture, food and manufacturing. This positive growth is going to continue in the coming years, and could be one of the best development options for SIDS in response to the challenge of globalization.

Tourism equals other competing activities by creating added value, but is much less destructive and disruptive to the natural and human environment as long as it is developed rationally and respects the carrying capacity of sites.

It is for this reason that the World Tourism Organization is promoting *"tourism liberalization with a human face"*, prioritising poverty alleviation along with fair trade and triple bottom line sustainable development. In order to achieve such goal, WTO acts in front of the World Trade Organization to make substantial progress in the way it deals with the complex, cross-sectoral activity of tourism. The World Tourism Organization is committed to assisting in that process and, as a new United Nations specialized agency, is well positioned for the challenge.

Only when the economic impact of tourism is fully recognized, will the tourism industry be able to gain in credibility among political organizations and international financial institutions. But at the same time, the tourism industry and those responsible for tourism in the public sector should also recognize that tourism can generate serious impacts upon the natural and built environments, as well as on the social fabric of island nations. The prevention and reduction of such impacts requires cooperation and continuous monitoring.

As highlighted in this document, there is no other complex activity like tourism that cuts across so many sectors, offering possibilities for increased linkages, but also risks in many areas.

Thus, because of its complexity tourism impacts and opportunities would need to be fully integrated in most of the other sectors defined in the BPoA: Coastal and marine resources, Biodiversity resources, Freshwater resources, Land resources, Energy resources, Management of wastes, National institutions and administrative capacity, Regional institutions and technical cooperation, Transport and communication, Science and technology, Human resource development, Implementation, monitoring and review.

The Johannesburg Plan of Implementation recalls in Paragraph 43 concerning Tourism, that international cooperation and partnership at all levels should be seen as a prime objective for SIDS.

Reducing small islands isolation is key to their sustainable development. Enhancing inter-regional and international activities can strengthen small islands, so that by working together they can achieve sustainable lifestyles, retain their uniqueness and individuality, and effect meaningful change for the benefit of their people.

The presence of the World Tourism Organization at the BPOA+10 in Mauritius is a step forward in the recognition of tourism as an important sustainable development option for Small Island States. In line with the above, the World Tourism Organization calls for the establishment of a **Small Island Developing States Tourism Observatory**, working closely with SIDS governments, with all UN Agencies relevant for sustainable tourism development and with existing SIDS networks.

The richness and complexity of tourism call for coordinated efforts by all institutions that deal with tourism at the international level. With this in mind, WTO undertakes to do its part to achieve the objectives of the Millennium Declaration.

Annex: Basic Indicators of International Tourism in SIDS

	ARRIVALS						TOURISM EXPENDITURE								
	1. Number (thousands)			2. As share of total Population (%)			3. Absolute value (US$ Million)			4. Average value (US $)			5. As share of GDP (%)		
COUNTRIES	1990	2002	1990-2002	1990	2002	1990-2002	1990	2002	1990-2002	1990	2002	1990-2002	1990	2002	1990-2002
ANGUILLA	31	44	38	371,6	373,0	372,3	35	55	45	1.129	1.250	1.190	..	..	..
ANTIGUA,BARB	206	222 *	214	328,4	290,3	309,3	298	274	286	1.447	1.234	1.340	..	38,0	..
ARUBA	433	643	538	649,6	662,9	656,3	350	916	633	808	1.425	1.116	..	48,9	..
BAHAMAS	1.562	1.513	1.538	607,2	481,8	544,5	1.332	1.751 *	1.542	853	1.157	1.005	..	34,7	..
BAHRAIN	1.376	3.167	2.272	274,9	453,7	364,3	135	741	438	98	234	166	..	9,6	..
BARBADOS	432	498	465	164,5	185,1	174,8	494	648	571	1.144	1.301	1.222	..	25,6	..
CAPE VERDE	24	126	75	6,9	27,5	17,2	6	66	36	250	524	387	..	10,2	..
COMOROS	8	19	14	1,9	3,2	2,6	2	11	7	250	579	414	..	4,5	..
COOK IS	34	73	54	186,5	357,7	272,1	16	46	31	471	630	550	..	..	..
CUBA	327	1.656	992	3,1	14,7	8,9	243	1.633	938	743	986	865	..	..	..
CYPRUS	1.561	2.418	1.990	229,1	316,1	272,6	1.258	1.924	1.591	806	796	801	..	19,0	..
DOMINICA	45	69	57	61,9	97,1	79,5	20	46	33	444	667	556	..	18,3	..
DOMINICAN RP	1.305	2.811	2.058	18,4	32,6	25,5	900	2.736	1.818	690	973	831	12,7	12,9	12,8
FIJI	279	398	339	37,8	48,4	43,1	202	261	232	724	656	690	..	14,4	..
GRENADA	76	132	104	82,3	127,5	104,9	38	91	65	500	689	595	..	22,0	..
HAITI	144	142 *	143	2,4	1,7	2,1	46	54 *	50	319	380	350	1,6	1,6	1,6
JAMAICA	989	1.266	1.128	40,1	48,4	44,3	740	1.209	975	748	955	852	16,1	15,4	15,7
KIRIBATI	3	5	4	4,2	5,3	4,7	1	3 *	2	333	600	467	..	5,7	..
MALDIVES	195	485	340	90,1	169,0	129,6	89	333	211	456	687	572	..	52,0	..
MALTA	872	1.134	1.003	242,8	285,6	264,2	496	572	534	569	504	537	..	14,8	..
MARSHALL IS	5	6	6	10,8	11,3	11,1	..	4	..	..	667	..	..	3,8	..
MAURITIUS	292	682	487	27,2	56,3	41,7	244	612	428	836	897	866	10,2	13,5	11,9
MICRONESIA	..	19	..	..	15,6	..	..	17	..	..	895	..	..	7,3	..
NIUE	1	2	2	..	..	..	..	..	..	..	..	..	..	..	..
PALAU	33	59	46	217,0	295,0	256,0	..	..	..	..	..	..	..	..	..
PAPUA N.GUIN	41	54	48	1,1	1,0	1,0	41	101 *	71	1.000	1.870	1.435	1,3	3,5	2,4
ST.KITTS NEV	73	68	71	176,3	145,6	160,9	58	56	57	795	824	809	..	15,7	..
ST.LUCIA	141	253	197	101,0	159,0	130,0	154	210	182	1.092	830	961	..	31,0	..
ST.VINCENT,G	54	78	66	50,7	71,5	61,1	56	83	70	1.037	1.064	1.051	..	23,0	..
SAMOA	48	89	69	28,2	50,6	39,4	20	45	33	417	506	461	..	17,0	..
SAO TOME PRN	4	8 *	6	3,3	5,2	4,3	2	10	6	500	1.250	875	..	20,0	..
SEYCHELLES	104	132	118	141,6	160,1	150,9	126	161	144	1.212	1.220	1.216	..	23,0	..
SINGAPORE	4.842	6.997	5.920	160,5	168,0	164,3	4.937	4.381	4.659	1.020	626	823	13,5	5,0	9,2
SOLOMON IS	9	..	..	2,7	..	..	7	1	4	778	..	..	..	0,4	..
TONGA	21	37	29	22,8	36,6	29,7	9	9	9	429	243	336	..	6,5	..
TRINIDAD TBG	195	384	290	16,3	29,4	22,9	95	224	160	487	583	535	1,9	2,4	2,1
TUVALU	1	1	1	10,9	9,2	10,1	..	..	..	..	..	..	..	..	..
US.VIRGIN IS	463	553	508	..	502,7	..	697	1.195	946	1.505	2.161	1.833	..	..	..
VANUATU	35	49	42	22,8	23,8	23,3	39	46 *	43	1.114	939	1.027	..	19,7	..

	INTERNATIONAL TRADE IN SERVICES												PRO-MEMORIA		
	6. Travel as share of total Services (%)			7. Travel as share of total Goods and Services (%)			8. Travel+Passenger Transportation as share of total Services (%)			9. Travel+Passenger Transportation as share of total Goods and Services (%)			10. GDP per capita (US $)		
COUNTRIES	1990	2002	1990-2002	1990	2002	1990-2002	1990	2002	1990-2002	1990	2002	1990-2002	1990	2002	1990-2002
ANGUILLA	85,4	83,3	84,3	84,5	77,5	81,0	..	..	..	..	..	..	..	..	..
ANTIGUA,BARB	95,5	68,0	81,8	86,4	62,0	74,2	108,9	..	..	98,5	..	..	..	9.427	..
ARUBA	85,2	85,4	85,3	61,8	35,4	48,6	88,6	85,4	87,0	64,3	35,4	49,9	..	19.330	..
BAHAMAS	88,8	92,6	90,7	74,7	69,9	72,3	89,6	..	..	75,4	..	..	..	16.083	..
BAHRAIN	37,6	70,0	53,8	3,3	10,8	7,1	92,3	94,1	93,2	8,0	14,6	11,3	..	11.007	..
BARBADOS	75,5	59,7	67,6	56,6	47,8	52,2	75,8	..	..	56,8	..	..	..	9.424	..
CAPE VERDE	17,1	43,1	30,1	10,5	33,8	22,2	28,9	65,8	47,3	17,7	51,6	34,7	..	1.406	..
COMOROS	11,8	..	..	5,7	..	..	21,8	..	..	10,6	..	..	..	422	..
COOK IS	..	..	..	..	..	..	..	..	..	..	..	..	..	..	..
CUBA	..	..	..	..	..	..	..	..	..	..	..	..	..	..	..
CYPRUS	62,8	42,9	52,9	42,6	36,1	39,3	72,0	47,8	59,9	48,8	40,2	44,5	..	13.210	..
DOMINICA	60,6	60,5	60,6	22,5	38,3	30,4	..	..	..	..	..	..	..	3.545	..
DOMINICAN RP	82,0	89,6	85,8	49,1	33,2	41,2	..	..	..	..	..	..	997	2.471	1.734
FIJI	48,4	..	..	24,2	..	..	65,3	..	..	32,7	..	..	..	2.205	..
GRENADA	59,4	67,9	63,6	40,9	46,0	43,4	..	..	..	..	..	..	..	4.000	..
HAITI	88,5	..	..	14,5	..	..	95,4	..	..	15,6	..	..	495	398	446
JAMAICA	72,1	63,0	67,5	33,4	37,4	35,4	83,5	77,2	80,3	38,7	45,9	42,3	1.721	3.008	2.364
KIRIBATI	12,5	..	..	9,1	..	..	25,0	..	..	18,2	..	..	..	558	..
MALDIVES	88,1	93,8	91,0	49,7	68,1	58,9	..	..	..	..	..	..	..	2.233	..
MALTA	66,0	52,1	59,0	25,4	17,1	21,3	81,6	65,2	73,4	31,5	21,4	26,4	..	9.748	..
MARSHALL IS	..	..	..	..	..	..	..	..	..	..	..	..	..	2.000	..
MAURITIUS	50,4	53,9	52,2	14,2	20,6	17,4	79,6	73,0	76,3	22,4	28,0	25,2	2.461	3.750	3.106
MICRONESIA	..	..	..	..	..	..	..	..	..	..	..	..	..	1.902	..
NIUE	..	..	..	..	..	..	..	..	..	..	..	..	..	..	..
PALAU	..	..	..	..	..	..	..	..	..	..	..	..	..	6.500	..
PAPUA N.GUIN	19,9	35,4	27,7	3,0	4,8	3,9	26,6	..	..	4,0	..	..	842	532	687
ST.KITTS NEV	107,4	53,3	80,4	70,7	35,0	52,9	..	..	..	..	..	..	..	7.621	..
ST.LUCIA	102,0	68,6	85,3	54,6	58,7	56,6	..	..	..	..	..	..	..	4.254	..
ST.VINCENT,G	124,4	63,4	93,9	43,1	46,9	45,0	127,1	..	..	44,0	..	..	..	3.307	..
SAMOA	55,6	..	..	44,4	..	..	60,3	..	..	48,2	..	..	..	1.500	..
SAO TOME PRN	50,0	76,9	63,5	25,0	55,6	40,3	..	..	..	..	..	..	..	325	..
SEYCHELLES	73,3	52,4	62,8	55,0	29,6	42,3	84,4	78,7	81,6	63,4	44,4	53,9	..	8.479	..
SINGAPORE	38,5	14,8	26,6	7,3	2,8	5,0	..	..	..	..	..	..	12.146	21.200	16.673
SOLOMON IS	28,0	..	..	7,4	..	..	32,4	..	..	8,5	..	..	..	564	..
TONGA	34,6	52,9	43,8	23,7	37,5	30,6	35,4	..	..	24,2	..	..	..	1.376	..
TRINIDAD TBG	28,9	39,0	33,9	4,2	4,6	4,4	67,4	66,9	67,1	9,7	7,9	8,8	4.229	7.187	5.708
TUVALU	..	..	..	..	..	..	..	..	..	..	..	..	..	..	..
US.VIRGIN IS	..	..	..	..	..	..	..	..	..	..	..	..	..	..	..
VANUATU	65,0	38,7	51,8	52,7	33,1	42,9	..	48,7	..	..	41,7	..	..	1.136	..

General notes

The figures indicated by 1990-2002 correspond to the average value of these two years.

* 2001 data.

Data correspond to the available information contained in WTO Statistics Database as of 10.11.2004.

Indicators: specific notes

1. Data correspond to arrivals of non-resident tourists at national borders.
2. The 1990 data on population of the country of reference corresponds to United Nations estimates. The 2002 data have been obtained from World Development Indicators database, World Bank web.
3. Figures relate to the credit component of the *"Travel"* item of the Balance of Payments of the corresponding countries of reference. This item is traditionally referred as Tourism (excluding international passenger transportation services).
4. Figures correspond to column (3.) divided by column (1.).
5. GDP data from 1990 have been obtained from 2003 World Development Indicators, published by the World Bank and data from 2002 have been obtained from World Development Indicators database, World Bank web. It relates to absolute value (3.) as percentage of Gross Domestic Product (at market prices).

6 and 7. It relates to the credit component of the *"Travel"* item of the Balance of Payments as percentage of items *"Services"* and *"Goods and Services"* in the countries of reference. In such cases wherein the percentage exceeds a 100, obviously is a qu by those countries.

10. Figures correspond to GDP data divided by Population data.

.. Not available

Source: World Tourism Organization (WTO)

Bibliography

Air Pacific 2003, *Annual Report,* Air Pacific, Fiji

Binger, Al 2004, *Potential and Future Prospects for Ocean Thermal Energy Conversion (OTEC) in Small Islands Developing States (SIDS),* Available: www.sidsnet.org

Chryssis, Ioannis 2001, *"Large-Scale Utilization of Solar Energy in Cyprus",* in *Toward 100% of RES Supply,* INSULA

Commonwealth Secretariat 2004, *Commonwealth Plan of Action Kuala Lumpur,* Commonwealth Secretariat, London

Eagles, Mc Cool and Haynes 2002, *Sustainable Tourism in Protected Areas,* United Nations Environment Programme, World Tourism Organization and IUCN – The World Conservation Union

Frangialli, Francesco 2004, *International Tourism: The Great Turning Point,* World Tourism Organization, Madrid

Intergovernmental Oceanographic Commission of UNESCO 2003, *Poverty and Reefs,* DFID, IMM Ltd, Exeter

Lengefeld, Klaus 2004, *Pro-Poor-Tourism and Sustainable All-Inclusive?,* Deutsche Gesellschaft für Technische Zusammenarbeit - GTZ (Coordination Unit Latin America & the Caribbean), Eschborn

Ministry of Environment of Seychelles 2000, *Seychelles Environment Management Plan 2000-2010 (EMPS),* Mahé

Prats. F. 1998, *Tourism, Environment and Sustainable Development in Islands, 15 ideas and 9 cases for debates,* AUIA

Secretariat of the Convention on Biological Diversity 2003, *Guidelines on Biodiversity and Tourism Development,* Secretariat of the Convention on Biological Diversity, Montreal

UNEP/GPA and the Global Forum on Oceans, Coasts, and Islands 2003, *Towards Mauritius 2004, Voluntary partnership initiatives from the 2002 WSSD and Small Island Developing States,* UNEP

United Nations Economic and Social Council 1999, *Progress in the implementation of the Programme of Action for the Sustainable Development of Small Island Developing States - Report of the Secretary-General, Addendum,* United Nations, New York

United Nations Economic and Social Council 2004, *Implementation of the Barbados Programme of Action,* United Nations, New York

United Nations Environmental Programme 2002, *Why UNEP is Focusing on Small Island Developing States?,* UNEP

United Nations General Assembly 1994, *Report of the Global Conference on the Sustainable Development of Small Islands Developing States, Brigdetown, Barbados, 25 April – 6 May 1994 (A/CONF.167/),* United Nations, New York

United Nations General Assembly 1999, *Addendum to the Report of the Commission on Sustainable Development acting as Preparatory body for the special session of the General Assembly for the review and appraisal of the implementation of the Programme of Action for the Sustainable Development of Small Island Developing States, Twenty-second Special Session Supplement No. 2A (A/S-22/2/Add.1),* United Nations, New York

Vellas, François 1998, *Report on air and land transport and sustainable tourism in islands,* WTO, Madrid

Wheatcroft, Stephen, 1995 *Aviation and Tourism Policy,* WTO, Madrid, Spain

World Commission on Protected Areas (WCPA) 2003, *"Recommendation 12: Tourism as a Vehicle for Conservation and Support of Protected Areas",* in *the Report of the Vth IUCN World Park Congress, Durban, South Africa, 8 – 17 September 2003,* IUCN

World Tourism Organization 1995, *WTO Seminar on Tourism and Air Transport, 9 – 10 February 1995, Martinique, France,* WTO, Madrid

World Tourism Organization 1998, *Final Report of the International Conference on Sustainable Tourism in Small Island Developing States and other Islands, 25 – 28 October 1998, Lanzarote, Spain,* WTO, Madrid

World Tourism Organization 1998, *Handbook on Natural Disaster Reduction in Tourist Areas,* WTO, Madrid

World Tourism Organization 1999, *Global Code of Ethics for Tourism,* WTO, Madrid

World Tourism Organization 2000, *Report of the International Seminar on Sustainable Tourism and Competitiveness in the Islands of the Mediterranean, 17 – 20 May 2000, Capri, Italy,* WTO, Madrid

World Tourism Organization 2001, *Report of the WTO International Conference on Tourism and Island Economies, Jeju City, Republic of Korea, 13 – 15 June 2001,* WTO, Madrid

World Tourism Organization 2001, *Report of the WTO/UNEP International Seminar on Island tourism in Asia and the Pacific,* WTO, Madrid

World Tourism Organization 2001, *Tourism 2020 Vision Volume 7: Global Forecasts and Profiles of Market Segments,* WTO, Madrid

World Tourism Organization 2002, *Tourism and poverty alleviation,* WTO, Madrid

World Tourism Organization 2002, *World Ecotourism Summit – Final Report,* WTO, Madrid

World Tourism Organization 2003, *Climate Change and Tourism,* WTO, Madrid

World Tourism Organization 2003, *NTO Marketing Activities Guidelines for Evaluation,* WTO, Madrid

World Tourism Organization 2003, *Recommendations to Governments for supporting and establishing national certification systems for sustainable tourism,* WTO, Madrid

World Tourism Organization 2003, *Tourism Market Trends: World Overview and Tourism Topics,* WTO, Madrid

World Tourism Organization 2003, *Worldwide Cruise Ship Activity,* WTO, Madrid

World Tourism Organization 2004, *Indicators of Sustainable Development for Tourism Destinations - A Guidebook,* WTO, Madrid

World Tourism Organization 2004, *Tourism and Poverty Alleviation - Recommendations for Action,* WTO, Madrid

Yunis, Eugenio 2003, *The importance of sustainable practices in the tourism industry,* WTO, Madrid